ıaı̈esı̈ ɑaı̈e below

CRITICISM:
THE SILENT-SPEAKING WORDS

CRITICISM:
THE SILENT-SPEAKING WORDS

by Eli Mandel

Canadian Broadcasting Corporation

PN
85
M3

Printed in Canada for
CBC PUBLICATIONS, BOX 500, TORONTO 1
by T. H. Best Printing Company Limited

This book contains the texts of eight half-hour radio talks first broadcast during March, April, and May of 1966 in *Ideas*, a program series arranged for the CBC Department of Public Affairs by Phyllis Webb and William Young. The talks were produced by Peter Herrndorf.

ELI W. MANDEL is Professor in the Department of English, University of Alberta, and has also taught at Collège Militaire Royal de Saint-Jean, Quebec, and at York University, Toronto. He was born in Estevan, Saskatchewan, and educated at the University of Saskatchewan where he was awarded an M.A. degree, and at the University of Toronto where he received his Ph.D. Critical and scholarly articles by him have appeared in a number of publications, and he is a frequent contributor to Canadian journals in particular. He is the author of two volumes of poetry, *Fuseli Poems* and *Black and Secret Man*, has a third volume, *An Idiot Joy*, in preparation, and co-edited an anthology of contemporary poetry entitled *Poetry 62*. In 1959-60 he was awarded a Canada Foundation Fellowship in Creative Writing, and in 1963 he was the recipient of the President's Medal, University of Western Ontario, for poetry.

AUTHOR'S ACKNOWLEDGEMENTS

It should be obvious at once that I am deeply indebted to many scholars and theorists insofar as I have shamelessly derived from them both arguments and content for these talks, and I must apologize to any who have not been given proper acknowledgement here and to all those whose valuable contributions to our understanding of criticism emerge in a distorted or contradictory form in my version. I should like to think the contradictions are inherent in the subject but I suspect that they are in fact only the product of my own limitations. I have to admit as well that I have freely looted some of my own articles for material, in particular, "Criticism and Creativity", which first appeared in Dialogue, "Notes toward a Theory of Cultural Revolution" from Canadian Literature, and "The Language of Humanity" from Tamarack Review. In all three my debt to Northrop Frye will be apparent, though the peculiarities of the argument are mine, not his.

In revising the talks for publication I have not substantially altered the style. It remains a combination of an address to an invisible audience and academic ruminations on the puzzles that academics seem most able to invent, if not discover, in criticism.

And I owe a debt as well to all those who listened patiently to the scripts in preparation, particularly Mrs. J. Rollins and Mrs. D. Sohn, who assisted, and my wife, who endured.

CONTENTS

I

THE NATURE OF LITERARY CRITICISM

A Time of Critics

Recently a historian remarked that he found no difficulty in identifying the literary critic because the last subject he would expect to hear the critic discuss would be literature itself. Psychology, yes; sociology, certainly; semantics, without a doubt; anthropology, inescapably. But a poem, a novel, a play, never. This is, perhaps, gratifying for a critic to hear. To say the least, it is more satisfying than the old cliché about the critic as parasite or the critic as insensitive, brutal, ill-mannered reviewer, a cliché perpetuated in more than one contemporary novel. But it still leaves us with a question about the critic's role, whether in the university, the literary magazine, or on the TV or radio panel, let alone in his articles and books which in our time have proliferated beyond anything Matthew Arnold could have imagined when he spoke of the age in which he lived as an age of criticism. And it leaves unanswered, too, questions about the nature of the discipline itself. Presumably, there is some point at which one would want to say that criticism is a major or even central social activity, and that it can be distinguished from literary scholarship, on the one hand, and mere book reviewing, on the other. Presumably, too, one would want to say that literary criticism not only interprets the art of literature but contributes to, if it does not inform, all types of critical activity, since one would assume that whatever it might be able to say about literature as a special use of language would in some way or another interact with and be a comment upon other uses of language as well.

These are some of the questions which I want to talk about

in this series on the nature and function of literary criticism, and it seems to me that they begin simply enough with the curious position of the critic, a position at best complicated by the fact that the subject with which the critic is most concerned is of all subjects most problematical. In fact, when we consider that he is surrounded everywhere by mysteries, the mystery of the creative personality, the mystery of the poem, the mystery of the reader's unpredictable taste and reaction, the mystery of the world itself to which in some way he must relate all the other mysteries, it is astonishing that he is able to say anything at all. And it may be that, for this very reason, he often puts on a peculiar mask. One thinks of Matthew Arnold's marvellous irony, for example; or of Eliot, who signed himself "old Possum" and who solemnly argues in at least one of his enormously influential works a sombre case to which he draws an absolutely incongruous and obviously intentionally misleading conclusion. If, indeed, there is an air of the charlatan about the critic, as there often is, it might just possibly have something to do with his sense that he is dealing with what, after all, is an illusion, or at least an illusion which presents itself as a reality that should compel and engage us and call forth our delight and even our assent. One of the most astute pieces of literary criticism, it is worth reminding ourselves, is Pope's *Dunciad*, a kind of non-poem, which surrounds itself with an apparatus of criticism designed by the author as an ironic commentary upon the non-creating word. And it was Jonathan Swift who supplied his own *Tale of a Tub* not only with digressions upon digressions, but with the anti-criticism that is the criticism which is, in part, the subject of the book.

The puzzle the critic must solve is that his first duty is to literature, and literature itself stands in an oblique relationship to the world and to society. He can no more break through its elusive boundaries with brutality and violence than he can pry apart a poem with a hammer and chisel. The cruder and more direct his methods the less appetizing his results. And in the face of, confronted by, literature, he learns something of the masks which he must employ if he is to enter that territory at all.

He takes up, for example, Mark Twain's *Huckleberry Finn* and immediately discovers that he is being warned off by the author, who threatens to shoot anyone finding a plot or moral in the book. But on entering the book itself he finds a more perplexing situation. The very first lines by the irrepressible Huck himself tell us that he is a character in a book: "You don't know about me", Huck says, "without you have read a book by the name of *The Adventures of Tom Sawyer*", and he soon discovers a dazzling array of books within books: the *Bible, Pilgrim's Progress*, the book of the great river itself, which Huck is able to read flawlessly, the signs and portents of nature at which Jim is an adept, and, above all, the romances of Tom Sawyer which turn a Sunday School picnic into a band of marauding Arabs; and at the end, perhaps with no surprise by then, he discovers that Huck has become Tom Sawyer and is living out a farcical romance invented by Tom. Obviously, some caution needs to be maintained in the face of the play acted out before him.

Or, to take an equally striking example: what is the critic to make of the deliberate shattering of illusion which marks so many of Shakespeare's plays? Time and again, at the height of his dramas, at the most perilous moment indeed, when what is called for, one would think, is the most utter solemnity and concentration on the part of his audience, the playwright suddenly and irrevocably shatters the illusion. At the pitch of eloquence in the last act of *Antony and Cleopatra*, Antony dead, Cleopatra herself in danger of being taken by the Caesar whom she now hates implacably, Cleopatra determines upon suicide, telling us she will not allow herself to live to see herself mocked in Rome by some squeaking Cleopatra boying her greatness in the posture of a whore. We are reminded, we cannot help knowing, that before us is the ambivalent actress figure of a boy-girl, herself queen and whore, telling us she will never be mocked by an ambivalent actress figure of a boy-girl, both queen and whore.

In these regressive images we are taken dizzyingly through a series of ironies that seem to have no end. What we have been absorbed in and moved by most deeply, we are now told, is only an illusion of an illusion, and yet it is in that multi-faced mirror of ambiguities that we are asked to peer most closely for an image of ourselves.

Criticism, then, occupies a strange middle-ground. It cannot address itself directly to the institutions and conventions for which it has come into being, since it then turns its face away from art itself. Matthew Arnold's ironic portrait of the sons of the earth should have laid to rest once and for all the ghastly desire of criticism to become practical action, to ally itself with a specific social or political program, or even with what today we would call an activist position, or to put away all nonsense about independence and intellectual delicacy in favour of a direct assault upon the remote ramparts of whatever truth seems most in need of immediate conquest. Arnold *should* have laid that ghost to rest, but one notices its dry bones stirring wherever a committee meets, whenever another conference of the arts convenes, and almost always on centenary occasions. It comes into being invariably at times of political crises and is, for example, the view of the more ardent of our own young separatistes and of the fiercer African nationalists, and it frequently makes itself evident in times of growing national awareness when anything like a disinterested view is likely to be regarded as traitorous, if not simply decadent. The temptation to join the throng, to speak the affirmative words, to reveal oneself as committed and concerned with the great movements in a society, is almost irresistible. It even makes its pull evident in relation to knowledge itself, taken in the widest sense. No one could miss the almost overwhelming demand for knowledge in our time and place, a demand that has thrown up across the country huge new universities and filled the classrooms with students, all apparently eager for whatever it is they are supposed to find in a university and clamouring not only for knowledge but for an active part in the administration and government of the university. No sensitive person could hear these demands without some twinge of conscience, some fear that perhaps he is not pulling his weight, playing his part, joining in the general chorus of forward-looking, optimistic, and absolutely loyal citizens of a great society. In this atmosphere, one might want to forgive the critic if occasionally he looks with longing toward at least the Canada Council, or to some organization to which he could attach himself with esteem, and there perhaps gain for himself, as a minimal gesture of commitment, say, the title of secretary-general or general-secretary. But as Arnold would have it, criticism itself says, this he must refuse. His task is to struggle, for the most part alone, with the means by which he might be able to say anything intelligent about the work of art itself.

There is nothing surprising in the view that criticism, for all its other aspirations, ultimately must, in Henry James's words, engage itself with, appropriate, take intellectual possession of its object. But when we look closely at *how* this intellectual possession can be achieved we find ourselves confronted by a bewildering number of possibilities. To see the object as in itself it really is, in Arnold's phrase, each critic seems prepared to don his own special glasses. The new critic wears a powerful pair of contact lenses, bi-focal for ambiguity; the neo-Aristotelian puts on a new pair for each poetic occasion; the Jungian's unusual microscopic refraction enables him to see what was never seen before: the invisible world of universal psychic design; and the Freudian's no doubt have sexual symbols painted upon them. We are no longer astonished when we are told that one of Shakespeare's sonnets has more than 4,000 possible meanings; we may shudder, but will probably accept with a sigh, the view that *Tom Jones* tells the story of Paradise Lost, or that it is essentially playing out a tribal initiation rite much like that which can be observed among the aborigines in a bi-sexual society; it may be something of a shock to be told that the white whale in *Moby Dick* is really Melville's mother, but less of a shock than hearing that Uncle Tom is a woman and that the relationship between Jim and Huck is suspect.

But if we are at all honest about our experience of art, if we have even for one moment committed ourselves genuinely and completely to a major work, we will not be taken aback by this diversity of critical interpretation and approach. The critic, after all, is one more reflector in the multiplicity and duplicity of the world of art. Both a puzzling and compelling figure, he is not unlike the con man or magician to whom he must pay his homage. Playing with illusions that are realities, dreams that present themselves as the waking images of the characters being dreamed, he knows himself in the presence of disturbing inversions, and the closer he comes to the paradoxes of that multiple world, the more radical the vision with which he is possessed. He might, then, like Henry James, tell us that all that matters is the art itself and any talk of "its representative character, its meaning and its bearing, its morality and humanity, [is] an impudent thing". (*The Art of the Novel*, 1937, p. 38.) He might, like Henry Miller, speak of the artist as "a traitor to the human race", one who "creates an impossible world out of an incomprehensible language, a lie that enchants and enslaves men" *(Lawrence Durrell and Henry Miller, A Private Correspondence*, 1964, pp. 46-67), or he might, like James Agee, insist that art is "beyond any calculation savage and dangerous and murderous to all equilibrium in human life as human life is; and nothing can equal the rape it does on all that death, nothing except anything, anything in existence or dream, perceived anywhere remotely toward its true dimension" *(Let Us Now Praise Famous Men*, 1960, p. 16).

And this is, fundamentally, the critic's dilemma: he must give to the demanding, insistent society about him an account of the value, order, and coherence of these tricks of the human mind and imagination. For this, and we ought not to mistake it, is what his society demands of him insofar as he pretends at all to social usefulness and significance. Condemning the work of art, both as a mere fiction and an immoral, wicked, sinful, depraved, and dangerous lie, the social world asks the critic to show that his concern is with what is uplifting, moral, affirmative, and healthy. Curious, but nevertheless true: art was taken to be both immoral and illusory by Plato's world; it met the same charges from the English Puritans, well before the revolution; and it continues to meet these charges both from the representatives of a decayed Christianity and the guardians of public morality, and from the rational-scientific-technological representatives of our own world. Historically, criticism begins as a defence of art against the double charge that it is illusory and immoral, and consequently, criticism has not been able to escape from the overwhelming burden of working out a theory of value or from the paradox that the only viable theory derived from the arts themselves appears to be subversive of the very forces which have brought it to an accounting.

In the tense business of value-judgments, we can see most easily how the critic is forced step by step away from his first concern with the work itself to another extreme boundary, a theoretical concern with the very grounds of his own subject. Beginning, in other words, with a defence of poetry, he ends by writing a defence of a defence of poetry, absorbed finally in contemplating the mystery of his own occupation. It is not difficult to trace out these regressive steps in criticism despite their apparently complicated path.

There are, in the broadest sense, only three kinds of value theory in criticism; one is imported from outside the arts; the other two are ostensibly derived inductively from the arts themselves. The imported one need not necessarily be gross, though it often seems to be nothing more than the imposition of external ethical categories and conventional wisdom. But even in its sophisticated forms, in which it derives subtle content from literature, it looks suspiciously as if it were smuggling wisdom into the writing rather than carrying it away. Needless to say, it has an honourable history; from Horace to Eliot critics have unashamedly extracted content from literature, though as Northrop Frye observes, any commentary attached to a work is a form of allegory.

The two theories derived from the arts themselves are the survival theory and the interest theory: one says simply the standard of value is survival; the other that what is valuable is what interests us; the first is Samuel Johnson's standard; the second, Henry James's. The temptation is to call these classical and romantic, respectively, except that the terms no longer mean anything, but it is worth noting that neither can be maintained easily without moving away from the work in question to a larger context. Concern with survival rapidly becomes concern with kinds of literature, while the standard of interest moves either toward a theory of creativity or of the reader's psychology or of the writer's personality. It seems impossible to speak of the value of an individual work without invoking at least other works of literature; ultimately, as in the neo-classic version, Homer, who is said to be the same as Nature. But as the young poet who himself coined the classical tag blithely asked, "When is a classic a classic?" In short, tradition is ultimately self-defeating as a value theory because it cannot forever conceal behind an apparently objective rule the relativism on which it is based. And the same, of course, is true of the marvellously evocative and passionate commitment to particularity in the critic concerned only with what engages and interests him. In the end, he must tell us *why* his peculiar experience is valuable, and he can do so only by providing a theory of perception or creativity which validates individual experience.

We find here, in part, the reasons for Arnold's increasing concern not with touchstones of value but with criticism as an "order of ideas", "an intellectual situation of which the creative power can profitably avail itself", and the reason why Eliot turned from a literary to a cultural tradition or context within which, presumably, value could be discerned. More comprehensively still, in Northrop Frye's *Anatomy of Criticism*, the whole of literature is thought of as forming an order from which, it follows, a systematic and autonomous criticism could be induced. In Frye's version, as in Arnold's, it is criticism itself which is the normative element in society, but it can only become so, if it becomes, in Frye's words, "the academic vision of possibilities which is the model of education". Unless we want to smuggle into criticism the illusory values of our actual society, it appears then, we must accept both the independence of imagination and the disinterestedness of criticism, with the consequence that, as Frye puts it: "The idea of a free society implied in culture can never be formulated, much less established as a society", though he adds: "Culture is a present social ideal which we educate and free ourselves by trying to attain, and never do attain." (*The Anatomy of Criticism*, 1957, p. 348.)

To put it bluntly: criticism inevitably becomes theory of criticism. The critic moves out from the work to tell us what he can about the effects created by art, about the relationships between art and the world it seems to imitate, or about the nature of the creative personality, and inevitably he moves through a whole range of theories in order to explore the psychology of the reader, the kinds and nature of perception, or even the formulations of a reality principle. He asks about the connections between art and ritual, art and mythology, art and anthropology, and so on through the whole spectrum of knowledge. In what sense, we ask, could he be moving closer to us by moving farther away? Is this what is demanded by the need to discover how an illusion could possibly connect with our everyday concerns? The only way to find out is to follow him into these dread regions. This is where we must go if we are ever to know whether the critic who leads us is pursuing a will of the wisp or a pillar of fire by day and night.

II

THE FORMS OF LITERARY CRITICISM

From Plato's Cave to Byzantium

We left our critic somewhere in the wilderness pursuing a pillar of fire. He had been led there, we might recall, by the ghostly elusiveness of his object, an oracular form as mysterious as a burning bush about which he is expected to say whether it is divine or merely gaseous. Having once bound himself to its mysterious ways, he discovered that whatever he might say about it, he was led to say more about why he was saying anything at all, so that in the end he appeared to be speaking not only to himself but only about himself. In this regressive movement into his own concerns, curiously enough, he is not so very unlike the object he pursues, an object which wraps itself around its own mystery and as often as not appears to be contemplating not the external world but its own being. And if the critic is then poised on a paradox, looking several ways at the same time, and hoping desperately that at least his mixed metaphors will not make him a laughing stock, he might take some measure of comfort from the fact that all this is a product of a society in which art itself is both a threat and an object of mirth. Yet the anomalous position occupied by the critic is something more than a product of social and moral forces. It appears to derive from the nature of the subject itself and the forms that subject then assumes.

The real threat of art, like that of criticism, is that it will dissolve the structures by which we form ourselves in the daylight world and take us into a realm of darkness and chaos where we confront not the assumed images of ourselves but those genuine and terrifying ones of the night world and the world of imagination. And most critical theory, in fact, struggles with this threat, attempting at one and the same time to hold itself within some Apollonian dream of daylight and order while revealing without surrendering to a Dionysiac night world in which anything is not only possible, but probable. These tensions are at any time capable of ripping a critical theory into shreds, leaving the critic finally silent in the face of what he has discovered his work is really about. Just as the poet is finally concerned with a secret, so the critic too comes into contact with the secret world, though his usual approach is analytic rather than ecstatic. In fact, it is primarily through an analytic approach that he can become aware of the nature of the tensions with which he is dealing and see that they are contained in his own work.

One of the earliest critical comments, for example, turned art into an imitation of an imitation of an imitation, and an equally early view said that, at best, the artist is an inspired madman, from which it follows that the critic himself could scarcely be sane. It was these extremes which were met by Aristotle, whose *Poetics* remains so extraordinarily influential not so much because of its insights into tragedy as because of its method. For it was in the analytic scheme provided by Aristotle that the possibility of systematic criticism as opposed to a merely impressionistic one first emerged. At the very least it made possible the means by which we could distinguish the forms of criticism and so understand both the direction and import of any given approach. It also enables us to understand the very considerable difficulty of bringing the arts into a satisfactory scheme of values and into the acceptable daylight of ordinary concerns.

If we adopt an analytic plan of the distinctions "already common to the largest number of theories to be compared", a plan suggested by M. H. Abrams in his brilliant study of romantic critical theory, *The Mirror and the Lamp* (1953, p. 6), we find four major kinds of poetic theory, each determined by the element of art to which it is addressed. Imitative theories concern themselves with the relation between art and a reality external to art; pragmatic theories concern themselves with the effect of art on its audience; expressive theories turn to the artist and examine his psychology or the creative process itself; and objective theories seek to focus on the work itself as an autonomous object, an artifact. Viewed historically rather than analytically, the scheme tends to resolve itself into a two-fold rather than four-fold division. On the one hand, Aristotelian or imitative theory views art as a product; on the other, Longinian theory views it as a process. The one is interested in the formal relations within the work and its existence as object; the other in the work as a mode of perception and expression, particularly of unusual, heightened, or secret aspects of being and personality. As Abrams has shown, the Longinian expressive theory became dominant in the late eighteenth and nineteenth centuries and has been associated with romantic attitudes toward poetry as creativity, imagination, organic growth, myth-making, and the work of natural genius. It has tended from the beginning to be revolutionary or radical in its implications, and to find its home among both religious visionaries and the disaffected at all times. The distinction between imitation and expression, in fact, appears to be a perennial one. It is fundamentally the distinction between closed and open verse which in Charles Olson's manifesto on projective verse presented itself as a new account of poetry; and in historical perspective, it seems not the least surprising to discover that Alan Ginsburg should have begun as a disaffiliated poet returning to the tradition of Whitman and that he should have moved from there to the mysteries of Oriental religions and the transports of marijuana. It is the same distinction which accounts for the perennial quarrel between the poet and the critic, the poet declaring himself in Nietzschean fashion an exponent of a transcendental madness in deadly opposition to what he takes to be the rationality, systematizing, and order of the critic. A current version shows up in a recent article in the New Statesman where the writer distinguishes between an aesthetic best exemplified by the form of a Chinese vase, and an aesthetic exemplified by "the skills of a light comedian who by subtleties of timing can make inert material live, and seem expressive of life". (Stuart Hampshire, "Henry James and Posterity", 1963, p. 639.) The fact is that however it manifests itself, the element of creativity in art has always proved a difficulty for imitative theory.

The impulse of imitative theory is to provide an adequate ground for the arts by equating them with truth to nature, however one interprets those menacingly ambiguous terms. But within any theory of imitation, there are always forces which push toward an opposite pole. If, for example, the nature which is being imitated is said to be empirical, the problem is how to account for those aspects of a work which obviously bear no relationship to empirical reality. There is no way in which, except by the grossest kind of allegorizing, one can assimilate Carroll's *Alice in Wonderland* to empirical reality. Nor will it do to say that the work recounts a dream, because one of its points is precisely that we cannot know whether Alice's dream is the actuality or whether her waking self is only a shrunken form of her wonderland. If, on the other hand, in order to account for those aspects of nature which are being defied or distorted in art, we say the nature being imitated is a neo-platonic world of ideal forms behind appearances, there is a tendency to locate these forms within the artist rather than outside of him. Art then becomes an internal imitation, an expression of the artist's powers or even an expression of his psychology.

The argument comes down finally to one worked out by Reid MacCallum in his *Imitation and Design*. There are religious, moral, aesthetic, and logical objections to the view that art is concerned with likeness or representation, and under the force of these objections art moves to a non-representational pole where the artist, as MacCallum says, "vies with nature, not in respect of her . . . products, but in respect of the creative . . . power she displays". (*Imitation and Design*, 1953, p. 21.) But if the motive in the development is cognitive, a search for true likeness, then the development is paradoxical. For "what it finally terminates in turns out to be decisively subjective: the primacy of aesthetic over natural form, of expression over representation, of rhythmic pattern over objective order and structure". (*Imitation and Design*, 1953, p. 32.)

Obviously, the critic interested in a socially acceptable criticism, or in the means by which he might relate his criticism to the adjustments and re-arrangements which he takes to be necessary to the health and vitality of a given system, will seek to work out and commend an imitative theory and probably along with it a pragmatic one. He is likely to be interested in purgative or cathartic images with the particular view of suggesting that by acting out the terrors of the known world the artist either rids us of these terrors or effects some mysterious re-adjustment within us so that our impulses are now properly ordered. He will pay considerable attention to the values of harmony and order, and perhaps make a point of noticing to what extent by representation the work of art calls our attentions to the patterns in experience which we are at least likely to observe. There seems no reason why, as a harmless exercise in essay writing, this sort of criticism should not be practised. It easily moves over into a kind of popular sociology in which we are asked to notice particularly the extent to which general tendencies within our society have been given lively shape and expression, and it provides a kind of case-book psychologizing as well in which we are allowed to find in the dilemmas and conflicts of fictional characters *exempla* of behaviour, good and bad, which we may or may not follow as we choose. To the objection that this is a caricature of the remarkably subtle insights of a critic like Ian Watt who offers an astonishingly detailed account of the connection between the rise of the novel and the development of empirical philosophy, one can only answer that novels are more than *exempla* of empirical philosophy. There's always Leslie Fiedler to show that they are really case books of Freudian psychology. The question is not whether sociological or psychological or even neo-Thomistic standards of reality prevail in the novel or poem, but whether any of these is in fact adequate to the tensions within the work or particularly to the mysteries of the obviously non-representational in art.

Clearly, at certain times certain theories will be more applicable than others. It seems obvious enough that there is an element of empirical imitation in the novel, for example, particularly in the individualizing of characters, in the specifically detailed settings, and in the arrangement of time sequences and causality in plot structure. But it is puzzling to discover, at the same time as the novel takes its rise, the obsessive concern with the theme of seduction, to which Fiedler draws our attention, or more puzzling to encounter work which, like Emily Brontë's, led Forster to speak of the prophetic novel about which he said he could not be humorous.

The relativistic argument, in short, answers only part of the question, and certainly provides no exclusive answer to the more urgent question of how the critic is to take account of the non-representational in art. Nor does it do to argue that this is an element peculiar to contemporary art. It may very well be that it has become more striking in contemporary art than ever before, and that this in turn is connected with peculiar historical and intellectual developments. There is no question, for example, that the ancient tension between poetry and fact, poetry and history, poetry and time was intensified rather than lessened both by developing creative theory and by the implications of precise thought in the nineteenth century. Geological and astronomical discoveries, anthropological theorizing, pre-Darwinian and Darwinian biology, the higher criticism, all combined to complicate the already precarious position of the artist. And utilitarian and positivistic elements tended to sharpen these divisions, as in Bentham's equation of pushpin and poetry, with pushpin proving more significant on the basis of a quantitative measurement of the pleasure principle. More people like pushpin, and that's all there is to it. And if we are to believe Marshall McLuhan, alterations in our own sense perceptions resulting from new media reflect themselves in radical alterations of the perspectives and patterns of art itself.

But the historical argument simply does not dispose of the basic nature of the tension between imitation and creativity. From Shakespeare's sonnets through to Keats's odes to the poetry of Stevens and Yeats, poets have put into opposition the world of generation and the city of god, the passing and altering, albeit deeply human, world of love and desire and loss, and the immortal forms of the created world of art. In the one stands the poet, as human being, a fool and lust-driven failure in Shakespeare's sonnets, a dying youth in Keats's odes, a tattered coat upon a stick in Yeats's "Sailing to Byzantium"; in the other world, the Olympian gods in a garden of perennial delights, the immovable and moving lovers on the Grecian urn, or the still sages standing in the holy fire of the city of Byzantium. The deep-rooted nature of the opposition and the enormous tension which it generates is immediately apparent in the extra-ordinary and ultimately irreconcilable oppositions contained in such poems and in the passion with which the poet dramatizes the conflict.

But the poet, like the critic, moves from Plato's cave to the holy city of Byzantium only at a cost. Imitative theory and pragmatic theory, whatever we might say about their ultimate validity or even the quality of their insight, do seek to keep the arts in some relationship with the known and intelligible world, with what an eighteenth-century critic might speak of as "just representations of universal human nature". They seek to find in both form and characterization the universal forms of nature and the quality and character of the human being, and they attempt to discover in what ways an audience is affected, alerted, changed, moved, by the particular work. But no sooner is the creativity of the artist taken as the standard, than any grounds on which art can be related to truth to nature are undercut and the ominous shapes of an unrealized terror begin to appear. The problem is one which Ernst Cassirer poses in his *Essay on Man* when he argues that art proves to be one of the greatest paradoxes for the history of philosophy, particularly in its creative powers: "How can we improve on our model", asks Cassirer, "without disfiguring it? How can we transcend the reality of things without trespassing against the laws of truth?" (*Essay on Man*, 1944, p. 179.)

The point is much more serious than an opposition between a naturalistic account or embodiment in art and an idealistic one. When Sidney, for example, spoke of art's power to bring forth a golden age in opposition to nature's brazen one, he still spoke within an acceptable frame of reference. Everyone is prepared to accept an ideal which presents itself as a larger than life version of either nobility or epic heroism. It is quite another matter when we face the reality of the claims which are involved in the extreme version of creative theory, when, for example, we discover that it involves a rejection of the social order and beyond this a rejection of the natural order itself, when it takes what can only be described from the standpoint of sense and experience as demonic forms: the cult in our own time, for example, of full genitality and polymorphous perversity, the equation of poetry and bi-sexuality, or altered sensibility, and the use of hallucinogens, the creation of the non-books of William Burroughs and the elevation to sainthood of Genet. What is the reader, for example, to make of Leonard Cohen's prayer to a junkie, "Alexander Trocchi, Public Junkie, Priez Pour Nous", in which we are assured none is so pure, none so innocent as the drug addict?

There would, perhaps, be no point in discussing aberrations if it were not that invariably critical theory must come to an account of creativity in its complete meaning. Half measures are not only cowardly but untrue. For the end of creative and expressive theory is simply this: everything is possible, and as Blake would put it, everything that is possible to be believed is an image of the truth.

It is not simply difficulties in theories of value which confront the critic. The fact is that even within the most carefully constructed theories which would validate art by asserting its naturalness or its connection with the daylight world and the social order, he has to meet objections which stem directly from the nature of art itself.

There is one way out of this dilemma, though it is a particularly perilous one. That is, to assert the primacy of art over nature, of imagination over reason, of the imaginative over the empirically-realized world. This extreme view, which is taken in its most radical form by Blake, has the virtue of both simplicity and coherence. But like most coherent structures, it fails to connect with what is most patently human experience. Part of its strategy, of course, is to assert precisely that ordinary experience is partial at best, a distortion of human powers, a fundamental source of evil. It involves an inversion of almost every aspect of human life as it is conceived in social and institutional terms, and it sets as its standard of normality, not the generalized account which is the one against which the particular experience of art is usually measured, but the far more rigorous standard of the imaginative vision of the genius and the total stretch of imagination of which he is capable.

The question is whether with such vision we have reached

the promised land or whether in our wanderings we have lost touch completely with reality and are now hearing only the ravings of a madman. And this is the question which criticism must answer before it can say anything of value about art in itself or as it touches on society and our daily life.

III

CRITICISM AND THE WRITER

The Mad Critics

It seems so obvious that there must be some connection between the writer and his work that any comment upon it could only be a truism. Yet there is no more baffling problem in criticism than posed by this apparently plain and open truth. And it isn't only the critic who is baffled and confused by this curious creature, the creative person. There he stands in our very midst today, welcomed as never before — or so we are told by those who feel the old tension between the writer and society has dissolved and that the Bohemian enemy is a nineteenth-century cliché. He is presented with medals and fellowships; he is courted by admiring and worshipful college audiences; he is poet in residence in some of our oldest academies; he publishes his letters and manuscripts before he is thirty, and displays with awesome frankness the peculiarities of his private life; announces his allegiance to marijuana or to LSD or to homosexuality, or lectures on his latest work in progress and the problems of the writer in a parochial society, or tapes and sells interviews at an alarming rate. Yet he remains elusive, ambiguous, puzzling; certainly, whatever else, someone not quite like the rest of us, always a surprise. It was one of our young poets who recently remarked on a CBC documentary as he was shown watching a monitor on which he is seen in a bathtub: "A man who allows himself to be photographed bathing himself is revealing less of himself than you might be tempted to think." And with a flourish, the monitored, half-naked poet scrawls on the misty bathroom wall: "Caveat emptor", which in his language translates as, "Look out, this is a con game."

Yet sooner or later, despite the obvious warnings, criticism turns to the writer and tries to say something about his personality and its appearance in his work. It seems to be driven to do so for a variety of reasons, beyond the obvious one that the kind of work he is doing can only be explained as an expression of his personality: perhaps because he strikes us as an unusually interesting person; or because he seems to be telling us about himself and writers generally; or because he is an extra-ordinary and challenging puzzle to us. But the insistent reason is surely that there is no other way to explain the element of creativity in art, and it seems important, especially in a society which daily grows more rigid and collectivist and in which personality dissolves into the blur of mass reaction, to account for the eccentric, the abnormal, the unusual, the exceptional.

It has seemed particularly important to provide an account of creativity since the early nineteenth century when the cult of personality in art developed and along with it the first Bohemian flaunting of bourgeoise prejudice and narrowness. Psychiatry itself, that science of the abysmal deeps of the human personality, is a nineteenth-century science, its origins as deeply rooted in German romanticism as in neuropathology. And psychological criticism is largely a modern development. Yet though the emphasis is modern, the problem is an old one. The eighteenth-century poet played some startling games with the masks of personality. We need only read Pope's satires to see the dazzling variety of poses which the satirist could take up. And it is worth remembering, as Donald Greene reminds us, that Pope spoke a language as immediate and dramatic, as fiercely muscular and "personal", as the language of the later Yeats. A standing joke of the time concerned the critic, John Dennis, Sir Tremendous Longinus, who thundered away about the sublime mysteries of prophetic art in a manner no romantic expressionist would be ashamed of. And Byron himself, the master of exploiting personal idiosyncracies, learned his art from that older non-romantic time. From its beginning, in fact, criticism has suspected that in the writer's complex personality lay the deepest secrets of his art. There have been those, from Longinus on, who chose to say whatever they could say about creativity in terms of personality.

Yet despite its long history and though the subject is a slippery one, in general there are only three kinds of criticism or critical theory which concern themselves with the writer's personality: biographical criticism, expressive or personality theories, and psychological criticism.

The most obvious is the biographical, obvious and sometimes vulgar. In the connections which it traces between biographical "fact" and a writer's work, for example, it is sometimes guilty of the most appalling oversimplifications: the suggestion that Browning's asthma accounts for his unusual diction seems to me unspeakably silly, no matter what a psychiatrist might make of it. This is not to say the form cannot be handled with beautiful and rewarding skill. We have the examples of Ellman's work on Yeats and Joyce, and Mark Schorer's study of Sinclair Lewis as evidence here, and too that endlessly intriguing and marvellous giant of biographies, whether fiction or truth, Boswell's *Life of Johnson.* Modern critics like to talk in somewhat lofty terms about the "intentional fallacy" which decisively cuts the link between writer and work, and there *are* logical puzzles here which are difficult to solve, but the instinct of the reader telling him to look for a human being behind the work is equally difficult to deny. So long as that instinct persists, presumably biographies will continue to be written, whether or not they do throw a true light on anything in the work itself.

A more subtle form of theorizing about personality emerges from those expressive theories which largely took shape in the nineteenth century: poetry expresses the poet's emotions; or poetry expresses his experiences, or his intuitions; his mind is an antenna, or a catalyst, or a sensitive plant; he suffers more deeply, or he sees more, or he is more finely organized than others; he records his finest moments, or his perceptions, or the drama of his life. Here we move from biography as such to a more generalized version of personality, perhaps the notion that the poet's mind is representative of the human mind at its most intense and fiery moments. From Wordsworth to Henry Miller and beyond, there have been variations of these theories played out, ranging from a simple-minded notion that the writer expresses himself to a subtle philosophical account of how object and person are fused in the act of perception. But for all their variety, according to one critic at least, these finally come down to only two modern versions: an intuitionist theory derived from Croce and Bergson, and a theory of experience derived from Dewey and Richards. And in his book *The Partial Critics*, this writer notices that all such theories suffer from the circularity of their argument: we know the writer from his work but we know his work from what we know of him which we have found out from his work. There are ways around this, but a more serious objection arises when we move still more deeply into the writer's mind, and it is this which we should consider, because its implications cut into everything we would want to say on the subject.

In its most startling form, personality or expressive theory becomes psychological or psychiatric criticism, more complicated, more disturbing, and paradoxically, closer to ancient problems of creativity than anything suggested by critical-historical biography. Of all forms of criticism, none is more easily vulgarized than this. In the hands of a vulgarian, it shortly turns all pillars, posts, knives, projections, knobs, and what not into phallic symbols; and to enter a room, it goes without saying, is a betrayal of a kind which hardly bears explaining. As for what it can do to "Red Riding Hood" or "Jack the Giant Killer", one need only read Erich Fromm's *The Forgotten Language* to discover, and to feel henceforth the story no more belongs to children than does that other Oedipal classic, *Alice in Wonderland*. Father figures lurk everywhere: we are told there are multiple versions of them in every Dickens' novel; and mothers, as cannibals or brides, turn up with equal frequency. Employed to examine the work as a case-book history of the writer's psyche, psychological criticism can quickly become a parody of itself, so that we seem to be reading a case-book history of a case-book history, as Leslie Fiedler undoubtedly would put it. Yet Fiedler's name reminds us of two facts about such criticism, as we find it in, say, his own work, or Ernest Jones's or Frederick J. Hoffman's: it does have something to tell us about the psychology of the individual writer, often something powerful and illuminating; but even more, it becomes a means of revealing the secret patterns of a whole culture, as in James Baldwin's passionate analysis of the guilt and neuroses involved in prejudice and in the sexual roots of the negro-white encounter in America; and though Fiedler's and Baldwin's cultural psychologizing, like much of this criticism, is often simply glib and more often gross, their sense of the duplicity of art, and of the paradoxical inversions by which it seeks to conceal what it most desperately wants to reveal, will not let the reader remain for long complacent in his belief that only the surfaces matter. *Notes of a Native Son* and *Love and Death in the American Novel* are what they intend to be, deeply disturbing works that tell secrets we would prefer remained secret.

The whole point of Freudian criticism, perhaps, is precisely here: not that it makes a case-history of a poem, but that it tells us, as Lionel Trilling argues in a classic essay on the subject, that the mind itself operates by means which can only be called poetic. The point has been laboured by many critics: the so-called "mechanisms" of the mind are in fact poetic "techniques". But few of the critics who go over this point, and over the various objections to it, have noticed the most fundamental objection, that insofar as we are talking of the operations or mechanisms of the mind, we are talking also of the operations or mechanisms of the unconscious, and this realm, whatever else it may be, is a night world, the world of the "id", the Dionysiac realm, that impossible urge always surging against the thin daylight layer of consciousness and threatening to break it into chaos and darkness. Insofar as poetry is the language of the unconscious, it is, from the point of view of the conscious world, the language of darkness, of chaos, of the impossible, in short, of madness. And here we are back to one of the oldest of stereotypes about the writer, that he is a madman. Paradoxically and by a most disconcerting route we come back to where we began. We discover that the element of creativity in poetry is a disturbing element and that it cuts poetry off from its one possible line of defence as a moral humane art, its connection with what we call reality or in the old terms, the nature that it imitates. For it is now the science of the mind that tells us poetry is a form of madness.

The stereotype goes back to Socrates and his comments on divine frenzy in the *Ion*, but as Trilling argues, from the early nineteenth century on, "with the development of a more elaborate psychology and a stricter and more literal view of mental and emotional normality", the statement that the poet is mad is "more strictly and literally intended" ("Art and Neurosis", *The Liberal Imagination*, 1953, p. 159) than in any earlier time. This characteristic notion of our culture, as Trilling remarks, is reinforced by the Freudian view that the artist is a neurotic who seeks in art a substitute means of gratification. And it gains impetus both from those who would attack art and genius as an aberration and from those who would defend its abnormality as a necessary means to and condition of exceptional insights. William James, for example, in his *The Varieties of Religious Experience* (1958, p. 31), cites some amusing examples of grossly materialistic accounts of genius. "Genius", declares one learned doctor, "is but one of the many branches of the neuropathic tree." And, explains another, "Genius is a symptom of hereditary degeneration of the epileptoid variety, and is allied to moral insanity." But this does not sound so different from those who defend the artist's madness, Nietzsche, for example, or Thomas Mann. Mann defends the Nietzschean position in a remarkable foreword to the short novels of Dostoevsky:

> The truth is that life has never been able to do without the morbid, and probably no adage is more inane than the one which says that 'only disease can come from the diseased.' Life is not prudish, and it is probably safe to say that life prefers creative, genius-bestowing disease a thousand times over to prosaic health . . . certain attainments of the soul and the intellect are impossible without disease, without insanity, without spiritual crime…

Here, at length, it becomes extraordinarily important to distinguish finally and firmly between the artist and his work, between personality and achievement. The defence has a strong case. Trilling, for example, argues that the logical flaw in the equation of an artist's illness with his achievement is simply that it fails to account for all those others who are ill and who do not achieve: therefore the illness could hardly be a necessary condition of art; and, like William James, he argues as well, there is a difference between origins and value. The man may be sick, but surely the characteristic of his art is precisely its order, coherence, pattern, and its relationship to a world which we understand or which is clarified for us by the work itself. The arguments are sound, but what in fact they do is, I think, precisely what the critic does not want them to do. Freeing the artist from the charge of insanity, they deprive us of the one means we have of explaining the peculiarities and distortions and *unnaturalness* of the work, and so we are led to conclude that if the man is not mad, then his work must be. This, in essence, is the origin of the stereotype of the madness of the artist, that his work transcends the natural and defies explanation in natural or common-sense or rational terms.

It defies explanations of this sort for two reasons, to which Northrop Frye in particular draws our attention: its formal principles are essentially and radically irrational; and it makes an insistent claim to inspiration. The first reason, then, is simply that in its metaphorical structure, in its use of metaphor, the poem presents us with statements, if we want to call them so, which are literally unacceptable. Metaphor, as Frye argues, states an identity. It joins what in nature cannot be joined. "Think of certain poems of René Char or Henri Michaux, Hart Crane or Dylan Thomas . . .", asks Jacques Maritain. Such poetry, he continues, "strikes us at the heart through forbidden ways". (*Creative Intuition in Art and Poetry*, 1955, p. 54.) The terror, the forbidden ways of such poems, these are the peculiar uses of metaphor in which the poet takes flatly as *truth* what we want only to take as *likeness*. In Dylan Thomas's "Ceremony After a Fire Raid", for example, the burned child is said to be priest, servant, word, singer, tongue in the cinder of the little skull, and also serpent's nightfall. The point of these odd identifications becomes clear when at the end of the poem the dead child is seen to be priest at its own funeral because the burning city of bread and wine is uttering a mass of water as the masses of the sea sound the "sundering ultimate kingdom of genesis' thunder". Nor will it do to allegorize the poem into a death-rebirth theme in which the child's death is a kind of funeral mass that heralds a new creation out of the flames and water of the bombed city, though that may make sense of it all. Literally speaking, the identifications are impossible. Rationally, they are incoherent, make no sense at all. There is nothing in nature to verify the poetic vision which turns a mass of water into a sacrament. What Thomas's pun is doing is to join what cannot be joined. As Roger Fry remarks, the artist's perception is a "biological blasphemy", and it can easily become what Mann speaks of as Dostoevsky's "criminal perception".

It would be easy enough to dismiss this poetic perception as, say, poetic licence, except for what goes along with it, and that is the artist's literal claim to inspiration, that which validates his accepting verbal associations as literal truths or vision. The claim is so widespread among artists and so insistent that it can hardly be ignored, though its precise character has not been noticed often enough. For inspiration is the sense that the work is given, that it has a kind of independence or separate existence from the author, that it seizes him and shapes him, rather than, as we would like to think, the other way around. "I dare not pretend to be other than the secretary [of my prophetic books]", declares Blake, "the Authors are in eternity." But as soon as this is said, we are faced with an almost insoluble puzzle. If we say that such statements are metaphors of creativity, an interesting manner of speaking about the process, we are involved in a contradiction, for we deny the validity of the experience we claim these words describe. We are left with one choice and one choice only: either we accept the poet's vision in itself or we deny it. If we accept it, we accept an autonomous world, one in which, as in dreams, what cannot be joined in life is there put together, one in which the impossible is the rule and the possible the exception. We grant the objectivity of creative art and if not the validity, at least the existence, of a vision of things so unalterably different from our daylight world that we scarcely dare contemplate its full implications. Jung, in an important essay, draws precisely these implications from the argument and points to the consequences for any theory of art or criticism. The creative vision, his essay implies, is not "something derived or secondary"; not "a mere substitute for reality"; not the outcome of a rich fantasy or of a poetic mood — that is to say, . . . a kind of poetic license"; not "an allegory that points to something all too familiar", but rather "the expression of something existent in its own right, but imperfectly known". ("Psychology and Literature", *Modern Man in Search of a Soul*, 1933, pp. 160, 161, 171.)

Grimly ridiculous, a crime against humanity, something that

"bursts asunder our human standards of value and of aesthetic form" ("Psychology and Literature", p. 157) — so Jung describes visionary art, and so he reminds us finally of where we have come: from questions of value, to the personality of the artist, and through personality, as if it were not really there at all, to the world of art itself, to the work as something existing in itself and defying our canons of sense and reason and our understanding of whatever seems daylight clear. Having come to this point, we have come again to the question of how we will read this anomaly of human experience and human activity, and what it can say to us. But before we seek answers, we can note how completely we are in fact judged by what we think we create. There are those who would evaluate art and its role in human affairs and society, and evaluating it, would say that this man belongs in our midst and that one does not. Such men often rise in our parliaments to announce that new horrors have been perpetrated on the network, that new obscenities or vulgarities have been allowed, and that the voices of our playwrights and poets and critics ought to be silenced. In the end, hearing those voices, some might be comforted to know that they do not evaluate art or judge it; rather, it evaluates them and judges them. Again, it is Jung who says what needs to be said, though he is here only echoing the poets who speak of inspiration: "It is not Goethe who creates *Faust*, but *Faust* which creates Goethe." ("Psychology and Literature", pp. 170-171.) "The artist", Jung tells us, "is not a person endowed with free will who seeks his own ends, but one who allows art to realize its purposes through him." ("Psychology and Literature", p. 169.) We may never fully know those purposes, or be able to face them in all their terrifying demands, or even understand why they are made, but we can be certain of this at least: they ask us to be more than we ever are in our own lives, and in the face of that overwhelming question we might be less likely to declare there is nothing left to do but lock up the eccentrics and pronounce sentence on all but our respectable neighbours, whose night-time dreams and terrors, after all, are not revealed to us.

IV

CRITICISM AND THE WORK

The Groves of Academe

The creative process remains a mystery, and the attempt to solve it by seeking out its origins in the artist's personality seems ultimately both illogical and futile. As often as not, in fact, the elusive personality of the writer turns out to be what the word implies: a *persona*, a mask or disguise. If we ask what it is that is masked, we find the answer self-defeating. As in the old expressionist story in which the ventriloquist becomes his dummy and the dummy the ventriloquist, the mask is formative, powerful, creative, possessed of a life of its own. Perhaps the only insight we can have into the artist's character is that terrifying one displayed by the brilliant mime, Marcel Marceau. Trying on the masks of comedy and tragedy one after another, shifting from one to the other at an ever-increasing tempo, the mimic finally discovers that he cannot remove the clown's face, and we are left to watch him as he struggles desperately to take off the grinning mask, his body contorted and grotesque in all the postures of a suffering, tortured man who must wear forever that idiotic smile he once put on for fun. He has become the mask he wears. But if the writer is formed by his art and must live out the images that possess him, if he is the compelled image, what does this tell us about the critic? Is he too compelled and possessed by the forms of his art?

The sense that a subject has its own laws and its own shape will be familiar to anyone who has tried to write serious work of any kind. It is, if we are to believe what they say of their own work, as familiar to historians and philosophers as to mathematicians and poets. It is surely related to the sense of inevitability in any urgent story, the sense that it must move to its predestined end and that any other conclusion would be a gross violation of the logic inherent in the story itself. Literary history, in fact, is strewn with the wrecked attempts of critics, and even the public, to alter endings which they did not like. There are alternate versions of *Lear*, of novels by Hardy and by Dickens, and some even suspect that Twain's *Huck Finn* is marred by the author's refusal to face up to the impossible conclusion to which he is being driven. From this point of view, it begins to look as if the formal principles of criticism ought to be located in the work of art or perhaps even within criticism itself. If criticism has a shape and coherence at all, if it is something more than the prejudices and impressions of the critic, it obviously will have to say something about the work as an art form and perhaps then about its own formal principles.

We have seen the reasons why the critic is driven away from the work toward other, larger structures. This is as much in the logic of his subject as any other development. But practical criticism, the attempt to interpret and describe the structure of a given work, is equally demanded of him. As soon as his argument leads him to the point where he speaks of the independent existence of the work, he is committed to an account of its nature. And if we decide there are analytic reasons for working out a theory of practical criticism, it is interesting to notice that there seem to have been historical reasons as well. Curiously enough, the history of criticism shows a parallel to its logical or theoretical compulsions as well as to developments in literature itself. In the early twentieth century, for example, there was something like a revolution in critical theory and practice, certainly in critical taste. As a result, there came into being one of the most powerful and in some ways the most pernicious group of critics ever assembled. The so-called new criticism developed in reaction to nineteenth-century expressive theory, in revulsion to the cult of personality in art, in an attempt to focus attention almost exclusively on the work itself, and as a rationale for modern poetry and the modern novel, that is, the highly allusive, concentrated, and often difficult poetry of Eliot, Yeats, and Pound, and the novels of Woolf, Conrad, James, and Joyce.

It began with a series of pronouncements that had about them the excitement of a new discovery and the air of divine or revealed truth. And for all its scholarly apparatus and sometimes complicated technical terminology, it has never quite escaped from its ecclesiastical tone. It suggests time and again that high mysteries are being revealed, that arcane knowledge is possessed by its high priests, that it can perform, if not miracles, the potent and proper rituals, and that it is an orthodoxy to which all must bend. Heresy, indeed, is one of its favourite words; heresy hunting its favourite occupation; and recantations have been known to take place.

I am not aware that anyone has yet told us anything about its vocabulary in detail, but it seems significant that one compendium of this criticism is called *The Armed Vision* and that the imagery of warfare—strategy, tactics, maneuvering—is as dominant as the religious imagery. Perhaps it thought of itself as conducting a holy war against the infidels, or perhaps it simply inherited from two of its influential founders, Eliot and Pound, the language of the bishop and the language of the crusader in the cause of culture. It was Eliot who, influenced by Irving Babbit's scholarship and T. E. Hulme's anti-romanticism, declared that the writer seeks to escape from personality rather than to express it. And in a series of shrewd and evasive essays, Eliot went on to establish a new literary tradition: the honorific names were now those of the Jacobean dramatists, Donne, and the metaphysical poets; the line from Spenser through to Milton and Tennyson fell into disrepute. Milton, according to Pound, was a lunkhead, and as for Tennyson, the less said the better. Pound himself, extending Eliot's interest in the French symbolists, argued for a tradition which would include the Provençal writers and take its forms as well from the Chinese ideograph.

In the work of Pound and Eliot, and in the tradition to which they refer, it becomes clear that one major strategy of the new critics was to isolate and distinguish poetic from other uses of language. They were followed in this, with bewildering rapidity, by a host of other writers, presumably because the distinction offered them the possibility of freeing criticism from those disabling concerns with non-literary matters which, in their terms at least, had prevented the critic from going about his real task. Obviously, if it became possible to speak precisely of a poetic use of language, it would be possible also to examine a poem in strictly literary terms, focussing only on the means by which so-called poetic effects were achieved. In turn, then, various writers, from I. A. Richards, to Empson, Brooks, Pottle, Burke, Tate, and Ransom, suggested or elaborated theories of poetic language, and we began to hear of ambiguity, irony, paradox, symbolic action, intension and extension, and the pattern of images in a poem.

They were, of course, excesses: Empson's dazzling play with the multiple meanings of any word could easily become and often did become a parody of itself, since he consistently ignored contexts and brought in as a possible meaning any meaning that had at any time been attributed to the word in question. In these terms, Gray's *Elegy*, for example, turns into a comment on the scholarship system in the eighteenth century; possible perhaps, but scarcely plausible. The mixed metaphors of Kilmer's "Trees", a favourite whipping boy of the new critics, became evidence of the poet's failure to control his material and evidence of his sentimentality and confusion; but for some unexplained reason, the mixed metaphors of Hamlet's soliloquy, "To be or not to be", tell us only of the over-riding power of the poet's imagination. Ambiguity or irony could become merely honorific terms, replacing those which an earlier generation had favoured, Coleridge's "fancy" and "imagination", for example.

No one has shown yet that complexity in itself is a distinguishing poetic quality, nor even that what seems to be involved in complexity, the reconcilement of opposing or discordant qualities, is peculiarly poetic. This in fact is precisely the argument which has been urged against the new critics, mainly by a splinter-group within their ranks who spoke of themselves as the neo-Aristotelians. This group, which did little honour to itself by writing in a horrific style, argued that there were logical flaws in the central attempt of the new critics to distinguish a peculiarly poetic use of language. The attempt fails to take account of discernible differences between different poems and different modes of poetry. It tries to turn all poetry into one kind of poetry, but it is really relevant only to a particular kind, the lyric, and specifically the modern lyric. It does not apply to, say, epic poetry, and because it doesn't we find ourselves in the ridiculous position of having to say that one of the major poets of our language is not a poet at all, a position which even Eliot found difficult to maintain. It is impossible to read *Paradise Lost* as an imagist poem, though the attempt has been made. It is impossible too to read certain lyrics — Shakespeare's songs, for example — as paradoxical or ironic or whatever is said to be the distinguishing mark of poetic language.

What the new critics were attempting, it appeared then, was to smuggle into criticism particular thematic or even philosophical concepts in the guise of speaking only about poetic language itself. They were attempting to construct a theory of poetry as a psychological balance wheel, a machine for ridding ourselves of unwholesome tensions or displaying the contradictions and anomalies of experience. But they were not, despite the claim for the opposite, in fact isolating and describing individual works in a way which would mark out their uniqueness and value. This the neo-Aristotelians claimed to be able to do. Their secret was to argue that a poem is uniquely itself because it moves by and is shaped by its own ends, its form, that to which all its parts are subordinate. Unfortunately, despite the logical neatness of the scheme, it broke down in practice, simply because it, like so many other neat logical arguments, is circular: a poem is what it is because it is what it is. So it was that the most elaborate analyses of poems turned in the end into astonishingly trivial conclusions. Gray's *Elegy*, we are solemnly told, is (1) an elegy and (2) the only elegy which says what Gray's *Elegy* says and (3) the only one that says this in the way that it does.

Any attempt to maintain the independent existence of the poem seems doomed to precisely this ridiculous conclusion, and the critic is once more apparently speechless in the face of what he most wants to be articulate about. Partly for this reason, much of the new criticism tried quietly to import wider contexts into its work: and from discussions of the poem as poem, we find ourselves led to that other extreme in which the poem is a disguised version of anthropology, or Freudian psychology, or

Jungian psychology, or Marxist sociology, or *in extremis* Christian theology.

There is a sense, of course, in which it is wrong to speak of the new criticism as if it were a single system, though one of its major impulses, expressed in a variety of ways, undoubtedly was to work out a satisfactory theory of language and meaning, and in this way to focus attention on particular poems. Its enormous influence and vitality derive from its sustained attempt to discover a means by which a poem might be read as a poem. And this might well explain why it so rapidly found its home in the universities. Brilliant, incisive, learned, philosophically subtle and almost unbearably sophisticated, it brought the critic into a position of power equal to that of the literary scholar. Its methods and techniques were practised by generations of undergraduates; it described, altered, and prescribed the taste of generations of readers; it determined the course of literature itself. But its very brilliance in part disabled it. For despite its very evident sense of the primitive and irrational qualities of poetry, it invariably turned poems into intricate structures of knowledge or at least complicated patterns of meaning. Whether or not this is a just estimate of its contribution is really beside the point, for the simple reason that this appears to be the estimate of both writers and readers today. And the evidence is plain.

The literature to which the new criticism paid its allegiance and for which it provided a rationale is now passing. The metaphysical or closed lyric, peculiarly suited to its methods, and the elaborately symbolic novel, to which it could apply its techniques, are no longer the dominant literary forms. They have been succeeded by the open poems of Creeley, Duncan, and Olson in America, by the deliberately flat and low-keyed poetry of the "group" in England, by the black-humour novel, and the non-novel, by the theatre of the absurd and the theatre of cruelty. De Sade and Burroughs and Genet are now the names to conjure with. The literature that went into the academy with the critics has broken out of the academy with an obscene shout of freedom, and presumably the critic too will soon be roaming the streets, or at least declaring in the academy that he ought to be roaming the streets. Perhaps his image now is the one we recently saw in a copy of Life magazine, the image of Marshall McLuhan, oracle of the electronic age, staring at a model of the global village and surrounded by all that Life offers: pictures of television sets with pictures of satellites on their screens, photographs in flaming colours of Cheese Enchilada, Macaroni and Cheese, and Cheese Haddock, photographs of black jets poised over what appears to be a flaming jungle, and sunlit photographs of a never-never land of tourists on vacation in the serene and incredible isles of Greece.

But the name of McLuhan reminds us that the form with which we are dealing is not lifeless and inert, but rather, as he would put it, an extension of man. This looks, at first, as if we simply give up the attempt to see a poem as an autonomous object, a created and independent existence. But McLuhan's remark, in fact, derives from a line within modern criticism and is very much part of the same effort to understand the peculiar, formative powers of art. His views take shape in the work of both Joyce and Eliot and are related, in a somewhat distant way, to the Jamesian notion of point of view. Once well into the thicket of McLuhan's language, the reader might despair of ever finding his way out, but the recurrent theme is essentially simple: that art is the language of the human body, an extension of man. The crucial point in McLuhan's theory is that the image we contemplate is an image of ourselves, of man. This at once takes art out of the realm of imitation, and because it does so, it at once accounts for the strangeness, the grimly ridiculous quality of art. For the absurdity in art is that, standing there, outside of ourselves, as a mask of ourselves, it is our own mirror image. It attaches to nothing objective, though it appears to be objective. It says nothing except that we are this image, though it appears to be speaking of worlds within worlds. This is, I think, what McLuhan means when he tells us that the medium is the message: form and content are identical; and the form is at one and the same time itself and an image of itself, that is, an image of man. To put the point another way: we are the images we create; we are the masks we wear; we are the improbable, unbelievable stretches of the human imagination that animates a world that could never be and allows all things to come to life and embrace each other. The language of this will be strange, one would think, only to one who had never read Shakespeare's *Midsummer Night's Dream.*

There is a curious literal-mindedness in McLuhan's approach which is one of his major virtues. It dissolves much of the obscurity that gathers about critical theory simply by taking as evident what is plainly evident. The puzzle about objectivity and subjectivity in art, for example, disappears as soon as we become aware of the fact that form is literally particular vision. This seems to be what Henry James is saying when he tells us that consciousness is form, that is, particular vision. What is not brought to consciousness, James would insist, is nothing more than a splendid waste; and it follows that the more intense the consciousness, the more particular and precise the vision.

The major difficulty in this argument is that insofar as it accounts for the uniqueness of form as particular vision, it seems to cut off the possibility of criticism in the larger theoretical sense and to leave us in the position, in which James finds himself, where we can say nothing about the value of a given work except that it is a unity. The critic finds himself once more in the position of having arrived at one extreme boundary of his subject only at the cost of having lost any opportunity to get to the other. Like the neo-Aristotelian view, the Jamesian seems finally pluralistic, and McLuhan of course is notorious for refusing to involve himself in value judgments of the forms he describes. The question we are left with, then, is whether in the view of art as an extension of man or as the language of the body, there is any informing or structural principle which would enable us to say anything about both individual works as such and their relationship to one another. If we are to believe Northrop Frye, there is in literature just such a structural principle, and it is evident in the recurring images and patterns of literature. Whether these ultimately find their origin in the mechanism of the human mind is really beside the point, at least if we mean to imply that either Freudian or Jungian psychology provides us with an exhaustive description of such patterns.

There is a sense in which art is a dream of man or even a sense in which, as Shakespeare seems to tell us again and again, we are being dreamed by the art we have created. But to say this is not to say we need refer our dreams to the analyst for an account of our Oedipal concerns, our fears of the castrating father and the devouring mother, our dream of an ultimate paradise of polymorphous perversity, to use Norman Brown's term. It is rather to say that we are creatures capable of imaginative vision and we have not yet deciphered all that that vision tells us, either about ourselves as we in fact are or what we might become.

V

LITERATURE AND THE WORK

Tradition and Pop Art

Every so often, when the mystery thickens and paradoxes crackle like lightning and darkness closes in on the long night of criticism, there comes along a sturdy sort of gentleman who seems prepared to tell us that we've been taken in by our instructors: there really is nothing to be so confused about, certainly nothing to fear; all will be made daylight clear in a moment. Such a gentleman usually proposes to speak in or for the voice of common sense; his method is an appeal to the common reader or to the plain facts or to the obvious solution; his tone, a mixture of bland reassurance and vitriolic irony. Recently, for example, George P. Elliot proposed to resolve all the paradoxes presented by the new criticism and modern aesthetics by the simple means of declaring that poetry does have a meaningful content. It is not about itself, as the new aesthetics proposes; form is not content, contrary to what the new aesthetics has argued; and poetry can make sense rather than nonsense. The paradoxes of the new aesthetics, Elliot snarls, are "mud, mud, glorious golden mud". "Oh let us never forget how much we owe aesthetics", Elliot declares, "particularly those of us who like to make mud pies, for it has provided enough and more than enough 24-carat mud for all. Especially irreversible-paradox mud."

Of course, everyone enjoys a breath of fresh air, and after a while the fashionable poses do become stale, the old arguments pall, the room needs a good clearing out. Perhaps one function of the critic is to sweep out the stale dust so that we can see the furniture as if it were new. But the trouble with the common-sense approach to the problems of literary criticism is that almost invariably it ignores the obvious in the name of the obvious. It simply is *not* possible to bring poetry into a simple common-sense relationship with actuality conceived in ordinary terms, for the reason that poetry is not actuality conceived in ordinary terms. And the critic may protest in as bitter a voice as he can assume about the mysteries and paradoxes of art and demand that art speak to him loud and plain and clear: it will not do so, or at least it has not done so yet.

There are two simple and obvious reasons why the language of poetry cannot be taken in the same sense in which we take the language of ordinary speech, in other words, why we feel that content is not relevant or that form is content. The first reason is that the words of a poem obviously must refer to a set of fictional beings or fictional relationships, however much we may *feel* that they are an imaginative re-creation of reality, or a genuine vision, or whatever honorific terms we want to apply to our sense that the work is overwhelmingly convincing and authentic. A favourite example of this quality of poetic speech is the ghost of Hamlet's father. There is nothing in the play that calls on the reader to believe in ghosts or to believe in the particular existence of this ghost; all that is required is, as Northrop Frye points out, a simple mental operation which all but the common-sense critic seem capable of, and that is, *supposing*. The language of poetry is, in this sense, conditional, or as Frye would say, hypothetical. It exists, even at its most serious, at the level of "let's pretend", and the only common-sense approach to it is to accept it as that. To do otherwise is to become involved in the ridiculous confusion of art and life which marks the attempt to find meaningful and literal content in art.

The second reason why the language of poetry ought not to be confused with the language of ordinary speech or other "languages" is that it is a conventional language. There are various ways in which this point may be put: perhaps the most striking is Northrop Frye's way of putting it when he tells us that poems imitate poems; just as you won't find a sonata in nature, so you cannot find the forms of poetry in nature; there is only one place in which you will find the forms of poetry and that is in the poetry.

I use Frye's name here not merely because, so far as I know, he is the source of these notions, but because I want to call attention to his criticism: the most elaborate attempt in criticism to account for the arts as independent of ordinary existence and yet as powerfully formative in social, ethical, and psychological contexts. Without violating either the integrity of individual works or the autonomy of art itself, Frye seeks to provide an account of literature which will allow us to speak of its social significance, its "ethical and participating" aim, as he would say. He is prepared to accept the paradoxes to which certain kinds of criticism commit us: that form is content, that poetry is most meaningful when it is non-sense, that poetry is about itself and is yet an extension of man. He is prepared to accept these and to argue as well that the one way in which we get beyond their apparent limitations is to see that literature itself forms a total order of words, a universe of its own, detached from ordinary experience, self-contained and coherent. There may be other ways in which it is possible to escape from the glorious mud of paradox: the common-sense way, or the way that rejects the whole apparatus of modern criticism, or by a return to imitative theory, or to odd forms of expressive theory, but none of these, it seems to me, is as interesting, as comprehensive, as relevant, or as free from objection as Frye's. This is by no means to say that his approach, by way of convention, myth, tradition, and archetype, is completely satisfactory. There are, as we shall see, objections, but none, I think, sufficiently strong to justify ignoring the particular insights and the peculiar pleasures which are the rewards of his vision of things.

Frye, of course, is neither the first nor the only myth critic in contemporary theorizing, but we needn't worry terribly about the others here. For one thing, to follow them is to move outside literary and critical theorizing into the bogs of anthropology and worse. For another, few are as coherent or as conveniently diagrammatic as Frye, who can serve as a summary of the approach better than any of the rest. His connections with Jungian thought, with the Cambridge school of anthropologists, with Frazer and Freud, and even with mediaeval exegesis and schools of symbolic explication, have been noted by others. But Frye himself blandly declares what seems perfectly obvious, that any one who reads, say, William Blake or the Bible will find the whole theory implied there. There's no need for esoteric knowledge at all when one is concerned with the elements of literature and the popular forms that literature assumes. Frye's use of the words "element" and "popular" is perhaps unusual. It is unusual to think of William Blake, for example, as a popular poet. "Popular", here, does not mean "what the public wants", but instead refers to recurrent elements in great art; it refers to "the art which affords a key to imaginative experience for the untrained". ("Blake After Two Centuries", *Fables of Identity*, 1963, p. 140.)

We come back, then, to the two fundamental notions on which Frye constructs his critical and literary theory: that poetry is a conventional language and that it is a hypothetical language. "Conventional" means popular or recurrent. It is convention which enables us to understand that poems imitate poems, for we see that the formal elements of art are purely conventional. The place where one sees this most strikingly is the realm of the stylized or abstract, that is, in those kinds of art in which there is least attention paid to the principle of imitation or to a reality principle. If we think of comic books, fairy tales, riddle, nonsense verse, or parody, or any popular recurrent form, like the western, or detective story, or the science-fiction romance (whether it takes place out in space or under water), we see what is meant by recurrent elements in literature. The characters of a western are not only repeatable and indestructible; they can with little difficulty be shifted to other versions of the western, for example, the adventures of the soldier in Ireland, as is evident in the way in which old ballads of the continental wars are transformed into western or cowboy songs, or the way in which the TV western like "Have Gun, Will Travel" keeps hinting at its origins in the romances of the knight-errant. The purely stylized or abstract nature of such art shows itself as well in its odd flatness and stiffness. It could hardly be accidental that the figures of a contemporary comic strip like Batman and Robin look peculiarly like the stylized figures in a Byzantine panel or like the saints and divines of a mediaeval triptych. Because it is form and design with which the artist is concerned and because he is, at best, only incidentally concerned with substance, experience, reality principles or whatever we want to call it, his work takes on the appearance of design, that is, the concern with pattern and not with depth. This is an art of surfaces and appearances, that is, forms. One wonders, for example, about the movement from myth, which dominated criticism in the early years of the twentieth century, to surfaces, which we now see manifested in what is called pop art. The great Campbell Soup Tin or the film strips of Marilyn are not content but design, the design of an age and the myth of that age taking its coherent shape. The movement from pop to op art ought to have been predictable, by the way, for the reason that forms have to be shown as appearance or better still, flux. Surfaces ultimately delude us, dissolve into other surfaces, change: and so the art of pop becomes the art of optical illusion, just as the form of a myth becomes, in a Shakespearean play, a shifting illusory version of itself.

In literature, convention shows itself most vividly in the most stylized literary forms or those stories, as Frye would say, which present themselves simply as stories. Myth is a story in which anything can happen, and therefore it is an extreme limit of literature, a structural principle of all literature which takes the shape of narrative. Equally, metaphor is the structural principle of poetry, because metaphor is stylized language, a language of hypothesis or identities. Those identities which carry over from one poem to another, or which are recurrent elements in literature, we call archetypes. And, Frye argues, the total identification possible through metaphor can take one of two extremes: a divine or a demonic extreme, that which is all we could wish for, an expression of completed desire; or that which desire totally rejects. It begins to look here as if the structural principles of literature, myth and metaphor, convention and hypothesis, originate in the mind of man and reflect the operations of the mind. In other words, it looks as if, in his view of wish-fulfilment and frustration as extreme limits of imagination, Frye is importing into his criticism the non-literary or extra-literary conceptions of depth psychology. Frye's answer to this is that studies of dream and ritual "can lead us only to

a vague and intuitive sense of the unity of the human mind"
but "a comparative study of works of art should demonstrate
it beyond conjecture". (*Fearful Symmetry*, 1947, p. 424.) The
abstract, stylized world of art, autonomous and independent of
ordinary existence, once more becomes here as elsewhere an
expression of or extension of the human mind in its imaginative
powers. Someone once remarked that the tragedy of Scott in the
Antarctic could not have happened had it not been for Conrad's
Lord Jim. Curiously, one supposes, there could have been no
Lord Jim had there been no *Othello*. The implications of such
a view for a theory of culture and for a theory of education are
worth looking at, but before we turn to that, we should look first
at the objections which have been raised to theorizing of this
sort.

Two kinds of objections are usually raised, logical ones and
empirical ones. Logically, the question becomes one of deciding
when we are confronted by metaphor and what a metaphor
is. This is something of a crux, not only in Frye's theory but in
all archetypal criticism and in all accounts of the imaginative
powers of literature. Admittedly, some attempts at archetypal
criticism are as silly as the extreme and vulgar versions of
psychoanalytic criticism. Simply to turn *King Lear,* for example,
into the story of Christ, or some kind of pagan ritual in which
the old king is slaughtered, is both silly and vulgar. More than
this, it is essentially a form of allegorical criticism rather than
a genuine awareness of myth as a structural principle in narrative and drama. It's difficult to say that Frye escapes guilt-free
here: after all, he tells us that the cave incident in *Tom Sawyer*
is a version of the dragon-killing story of old romance. But the
point is not in the application so much as in the method or
argument itself. Does metaphor imply identities which cannot
be found in nature or merely likeness which can be deduced by
a careful consideration of what is being compared to what? So
long as we talk only about metaphor we are in some difficulty,
but when we turn to fairy tales and other abstract forms, the
difficulty is to show that these do connect with actuality. The
only way in which this can be done, it seems to me, is by a gross
piece of allegorizing, the kind of thing done to children's stories
by moralizers, puritans, school teachers, and all those others in

whom the imaginative powers have long dried up and blown away, like a pathetic dust cloud. *Cinderella*, for example, according to one nineteenth-century critic, taught nothing but the worst effects of jealousy, and envy, and hatred, and especially hatred of mothers in law; and another critic, no one else but the great George Cruikshank, saw in the *Cinderella* story an opportunity to press home a temperance lesson: when the prince had found his lady of the glass slipper, a great party was held in the kingdom, and to supply the fuel for a massive bonfire, all the spirits and liquor in the kingdom were brought together and heaped into the flames, accomplishing at one and the same time a celebration and prohibition — and, one sadly notes, the death of another fairy tale.

Perhaps it is with the children that the answer lies. If we look not only at fairy tales, which after all the children took over from adults, but at their own literature, the sort of chants and songs and games and riddles which we find in Opie's *Lore and Language of Schoolchildren*, we find an art which is completely detached from the actual, perhaps nowhere more clearly than in nonsense verse and in riddle. Nonsense verse and riddle, we note by the way, are those elements of poetry which Frye speaks of as babble and doodle, or charm and riddle. The Opies point out that punning riddles contain "a verbal duplicity, implying . . . animate movement in an inanimate object" and a true riddle is defined as "a composition in which some creature or object is described in an intentionally obscure manner, the solution fitting all the characteristics of the description in question, and usually resolving a paradox". (*The Lore and Language of Schoolchildren*, 1959, pp. 74, 78.) The riddle, in other words, turns in on itself and does not face out to the world at all. If we think of riddle as a form of metaphor, then we can well ask about the language which makes of a candle a little girl in a white petticoat, or of a ring a bottomless vessel to put flesh and blood in. Of these, their own examples, the Opies comment: "Such images are, perhaps, the fittest introduction to poetry that a child can have." (*The Lore and Language of Schoolchildren*, p. 76.) The child's obvious preference for this kind of abstract art makes sense of Frye's contention that literary education ought to begin with the Bible and classical mythology and that it ought to be concerned with structural principles rather than emotional orgies.

But, the logician might press on, does not this theory reduce all literature to one kind of literature? Is it not reductive theory? The answer, I suppose, is yes. There seems no other way in which anything like a coherent theory of literature can be evolved and following it a coherent theory of criticism. If we rest with a pluralistic account then we will not have criticism in any valid or objective sense. Objective, of course, is a word at which some will bristle. They are the ones who feel that Frye is trying to turn criticism into a science and thus to rob it of all its glories as an art. The answer here would appear to be simply that the distinction between science and art on such terms is about as sensible as the one between the two cultures which Sir Charles Snow attempted to maintain. On the one hand, art, as Frye insists again and again, is not simply a warm emotional bath; nor equally, on the other, is science something cold and remote and mercilessly materialistic.

If indeed it were, then one would not expect to hear, as we do, scientists speaking of elegant solutions to problems, elegant ones being preferable, one assumes, to those which are not so elegant. But elegant is an aesthetic term, and one which tempts me to say the virtue of Frye's system is that it is a good deal more elegant than many others which I have encountered, particularly the systems of common-sense critics who offend with their vulgar and crude machines for pressing meaning out of poems. I would rather stamp on the poems in the hope they might yield wine.

An empirical objection to myth criticism is, however, more difficult to meet. It has to do primarily with the insistence in this theory that it is art itself, rather than individual works as such, which is the formative power in society. Empirically, we can ask whether art has in fact always served as a formative power in society, and if it has done so, what has it formed? What of the great periods of artistic production, the Elizabethan age, for example, or the age of the Renaissance in Italy? What sort of relationship between art and society is postulated here? And how is it that if the arts do not progress, as the sciences are said to do, but simply show us the vision of what we might become, that after twenty centuries of such vision we have become, or so some would argue, not less but more murderous, not more but less civilized and cultivated? It always seems a mistake either to grant too great a formative power to the arts as such or to postulate too close a relationship between a given society and the art which is produced by or produces it. Yet insofar as the myth-making or archetypal theory of Frye speaks of literature as demonstrating beyond conjecture the unity of the human mind, it suggests a wholeness or completeness of vision in literature which ought to have revolutionary effects on anyone who has become aware of it. Indeed, Frye, I believe, would argue precisely this, pointing of course to the work of William Blake and to the completed vision of the Bible as examples of revolutionary and complete visions which could transform any individual who is able to seize them in their completeness. I once wrote of Frye's work as "Notes toward a Theory of Cultural Revolution", and observed then that provincialism having something to do with boundaries, the worst kind of provincialism would be the limitation of the boundaries of criticism to unsystematic impressionism, the failure to enter into the great civilizing world of myth and concept; and certainly if we cannot say that the arts are a civilizing force we can say the opposite: that to do without them is to be less than human. There's a remark of Frye's worth quoting here: "A public that tries to do without criticism, and asserts that it knows what it wants or likes, brutalizes the arts and loses its cultural memory. Art for art's sake is a retreat from criticism which ends in an impoverishment of civilized life itself. The only way to forestall the work of criticism is through censorship, which has the same relation to criticism that lynching has to justice." (*Anatomy of Criticism*, p. 4.)

There are times, reading Frye, or entering the world of myth which is opened by his criticism and that of others who ought really to be given credit too, that one feels one has entered a dark world rather than a light one. The myths speak of sub-human forces; the stories tell us of cannibalism and the dark deeds which lie at the beginning of man's history. Who could read the terrible Agamemnon story, for example, without a shudder at the dread and fiendish powers revealed there and the inscrutable working out of a destiny for man that he might well wish were otherwise? Is this the glory of art which one had been told of? Are these the sunlit fields of Greece where the great heroes walked? And what dark values are being revealed to us in a world that refuses to be bound by human limitations? Surely, going into such a world, we enter that hubristic realm where, thinking we have become gods, we might perpetrate any horror. The mythmakers take us for once and all out of the daylight world and force us then back to the questions with which we began these talks: the question not only of the value of individual works but of art itself; the question of the morality of art; of literature and its responsibility or irresponsibility to a society that prides itself on its common sense, its practicality, its workable conventions, and its grasp of pragmatic if not visionary reality. Which is the 24-carat mud? The paradoxes of art and criticism or the paradoxes of a common-sense world throttling itself in the name of common sense?

VI

CRITICISM AND MORALITY

Oh, Sweet Delight

Throughout this series we have been dodging around a most perplexing question, one which becomes more pressing the more we talk about criticism. It has to do with the curious and troublesome fact that our obvious pleasure in making up and reading stories somehow takes us into forbidden places. Now, I think there can be no doubt of the pleasure we find in stories. We may moralize them. We may find serious lessons in them for living. But we return to them not because of any moral reasons or for serious instruction but because we find them fascinating, compelling, enchanting. And the elaborate structure of analysis which criticism builds is based finally on this most fragile of foundations, that we are interested, charmed, delighted by the imitation life acting itself out in words or by the world that could never be, that words construct for us. As soon as we realize that with words alone we can move out of the realm of law and causality, beyond the strictures of what we like to call reality, we find ourselves facing the central puzzle in critical theory: are there no limits then to what we might pretend in literature? Is there no danger to the individual, to the reader, in this realm of fantasy? Surely, we might at least say, there are better, more serious, more pressing demands to which we ought to give ourselves, and surely any claim that literature has to a central position in our scheme of things cannot be maintained if it is really nothing more than idle fancy or play, the sort of thing which might occupy children in their free time, or take grandmothers away from their brooding about the years that were and the bleak dying days ahead. Yet if this is merely idle play, why do we hear premiers and ministers of education and parliamentarians telling us again and again that we are in imminent danger of losing whatever morality we have left if we continue to read the wicked and depraved books everywhere available to us now? How can the imaginary, the plaything of children and grandmothers, be a threat to our society, our moral fibre, the very structure of our solid and respectable and infinitely productive society?

Traditionally, criticism answers questions about literature and morality in a variety of complicated ways, some so complicated that the sweet delight with which we begin disappears in a fog of argument and a great dust-storm of theory. And these answers are so complicated that I have no intention whatever of trying to trace out their intricate paths and patterns in this talk. Instead, I want to suggest simply one line of argument which, I think, at least says something about the sources of delight and the reasons why there are so many enemies of delight and therefore enemies of literature.

I begin with the notion to which a theory like Northrop Frye's leads us, that literature presents us with an autonomous world, a world separate from and detached from actuality, the world of imagination, and from this notion I want to come back finally to the way in which the imaginative interacts with and can be said to form the actual. To get to Frye's imaginative world, we have first to dispose of another argument. This is the one which pretends that there is something called aesthetic judgment and aesthetic value. It says, simply enough, that ordinary standards of morality do not apply to works of literature because all that we can say of such works is that they are either good or bad in purely aesthetic terms; that is, they are either good or bad works of art, and if they are good, then they cannot be said to be morally bad. All that an artist is required to do is write well, and beyond that he has no responsibility to his society, morality, humanity or what not. We have met this argument before. It seems to be what Henry James, for example, is saying, or what Henry Miller is saying, and it certainly seems to be what is said in defence of those works which have offended the captains of social morality. How often have we heard this defence: it may be offensive, it may be disturbing to the casual or ordinary reader, but it is an honest work and it is, you must admit, well-written. Since it is well-written you really ought not to say that it is wicked. Well, this defence, I submit, is specious. All aesthetic judgments seem to me to be moral judgments in disguise, and I cannot understand how it is possible to say that good writing is good writing without invoking some moral notion. It may be honesty, or sincerity, or complexity, or compassion, or purity, but whatever it is it will in fact involve a morality of one kind or another. And I fail to see why a dishonest, insincere, simple-minded, and cruel writer might not be one who delights us or compels us. I think of the Marquis de Sade, for example, whose vision of life is surely repulsive, or Genet, whose saintliness seems to me at least questionable, and yet I am not able to deny them their power and fascination as writers. Nor can I understand either the grounds on which we might want to deny them the right to be heard or the grounds on which we would deny them their obvious literary virtues.

The point surely is that when we judge any writer in aesthetic or moral terms we have somehow got the case, to begin with at least, turned around. If I understand Northrop Frye at all, he tells us that we do not judge literature, but rather that it judges us. This is not so very different from Matthew Arnold's statement that at bottom literature is a criticism of life, or Lionel Trilling's view that we do not read a work of literature, it reads us. If literature is imaginative it dwells not in the actual world but in a realm of possibilities, and the possible is finally a criticism of the actual. What might be, is a criticism of what is. What we can imagine tells us most vividly how shrunken and dismal we have become, and how we have limited ourselves, or how we are limited by the laws we assume to be the laws of our nature and of our being. We need think here only of the marvellous Olympian gods of Greece who, as Nietzsche said, made theology human by living our own lives, and we need ask only in what sense we tell stories of the gods if it is not to remind ourselves of our own limitations and of both the danger of transgressing those limitations and of forgetting that we are less than human if we fail to make the attempt. Or, if we choose to approach the question from another angle, we might ask ourselves about the meaning of fantasy, the fantasy of *Alice in Wonderland*, for example.

A child falls into a garden world where peculiar beings rush about according to the rules and whims of their world, where everything, from children's songs and poems to notions of time and space, becomes a parody of a pattern to which we have become accustomed, and where the most illogical arguments serve to support in an apparently logical way the most illogical conclusions to which this kind of reason invariably drives the logician. If the sane child Alice is mad, then what conclusions are we to reach about the mad animals and cards and adults who apparently are sane? If Alice is dreaming, then what conclusions can we reach about the world to which she finally wakes? Is the daylight world a shrunken form of the wonderland dream? There are no answers to the marvellous logical-illogic of Carroll's creation but there are haunting questions which will remain with anyone who has read that dream with any attention and care at all. Has he been telling us something about the reason in madness and the madness in reason? And if Alice has woken indeed to reality, then what infinite pathos there must be in her return from the wonderland where she alone spoke with the wisdom that everyone else would deny. It would be, I think, a mistake to miss the pathos which underlies and informs the nonsense of the child's book, just as it underlies all nonsense, just as it underlies that figure who of all figures is the most radical critic of life we have yet created, the figure of the clown.

It was James Agee who observed in a brilliant review of Chaplin's film, *Monsieur Verdoux*, that in Verdoux, the murderer, Chaplin had created an image of the respectable citizen against whom we are compelled to place what Agee calls "the most truly humane and most nearly complete among the religious figures our time has evolved", Chaplin's tramp, "that anarchic and immortal lily of the field". (*Agee on Film*, 1964, p. 262.)

From Shakespeare's *King Lear* to the limericks of Edward Lear, the clown in his mournful way talks to us about the tragicomic inversions of reason and madness, of sight and blindness, of ignorance and self-knowledge. Everywhere in Edward Lear's

nonsense poetry and limericks, for example, we encounter the
figure of the ugly old man, patiently enduring the insults of a
world which will not yield to his whims, sitting on a gate and
smiling hopefully at a hideous cow who will not go away,
puzzling over the oddity of a bird which is four times larger
than the bush in which it is hidden, and with infinite resigna-
tion putting up with the indignities of a nature that finds his
beard a nesting place:

> There was an Old Man with a beard,
> Who said, 'It is just as I feared! —
> Two Owls and a Hen,
> Four Larks and a Wren,
> Have all built their nests in my beard!'

At the end of Shakespeare's last play, the artist-magician
Prospero has put away his magical powers, and in the last words
of the play he steps out of the play itself to speak to the audience.
What he has abandoned he now puts into our hands and in our
trust. His puns and plays upon words tell us that he is asking
for our applause for his performance, but the magical words he
speaks tells us something more: that though the cloud-capped
towers and players have disappeared, just as he has foretold,
they now remain forever as powers of the human mind with
which we may do as we will. It is our decision. He has done what
he can and what he was indeed forced to do. Like the clown,
the magician-artist tells us we have been judged by the voice
of our own imagination, and just as the fool disappears from
the play *King Lear* when the old king wakens to his new vision
of things, so the artist disappears at precisely the same point.
When Lear awakens from his madness, he believes himself to
be with a soul in bliss, but what he now says to his daughter
remains the most penetrating and terrible summary of the
human condition ever uttered in any drama. One critic, with
an irony I doubt he intends, tells us that Lear's words show him
to be old, and foolish, and senile, and that we see the old king
relapsing into childish ways of thinking and feeling. I suppose
childish is the right word, for like the Chaplin clown or tramp,
the old king puts into opposition for us the great systems of the
world and the free, gay, independent, irresponsible life of the
lily of the field. Hearing his words we think of the tramp, pur-

sued forever down dusty highways and through the streets of the great cities by hordes of policemen with their clubs and cars, intent on only one thing, to capture the little man and put him away forever:

> Come, let's away to prison
> We two alone will sing like birds in the cage:
> When thou dost ask me blessing, I'll kneel down
> And ask of thee forgiveness; so we'll live
> And pray and sing and tell old tales and laugh
> At guilded butterflies and hear poor rogues
> Talk of court news; and we'll talk with them too,
> And take upon us the mystery of things
> As if we were God's spies, and we'll wear out
> In a wall'd prison, packs and sects of great ones
> That ebb and flow by the moon.

The mad king who has been blind now sees and is sane but his seeing-sanity inverts the world he has known: in the power of the court he found only a prison; in the prison to which he must now go he finds freedom; the kingdom he abandons he discovered to be the realm of human-beasts; his full humanity he now believes he will find in the kingdom to which he now goes. And these inversions, Lear tells us, are in some sense divine, the mystery of things which he and his daughter will take upon themselves as God's spies.

We may choose to read Lear's speech as we will, but it is worth noting that Robert Browning read it as an allegory of the poetic process and the nature of poetry. In his *How It Strikes a Contemporary* he tells us the poet is God's spy who, like the rogue-painter Fra Lippo Lippi, takes upon himself the mystery of things. But as Lippo reminds us, the mystery of things is a mystery only to those who dwell among abstractions, those who would deny the body and human desire, and those who would have us find a language for what we cannot perceive and have never known. To be a spy of God, then, is to move feelingly and alive among and through *things*, to come into the realm of being out of the mad realm of appearance and delusions. And precisely at this point the imaginative world connects in a most surprising way with the world of actuality, commenting on appearances by means of illusion. Fra Lippo's words provide the commentary we want and at the same time a defence of the morality of art:

> we're made so that we love
> First when we see them painted, things we have passed
> Perhaps a hundred times nor cared to see;
> And so they are better, painted — better to us
> Which is the same thing.

He is defending an art which has been called immoral and he must show that his opponents have got it all backwards. They have confused vision with abstraction and would remove from art its essential feature, its power and motive, human desire. Art, we may say, is the human form of desire. Browning himself spoke of it as a visible wish. And if this is so, then its mystery, the sense that it is detached from existence, can only mean that in some way we find the wish or desire inadmissible. We may choose to deny its admissibility on empirical grounds: "things are not what they are / when they're played on the blue guitar"; perception is no more than a ghostly spume, a play of appearance on the mirror of the mind; or we may deny it on moral grounds: surrender to a wish-fulfilment dream can only lead to anarchy and chaos. But we should be clear about what it is that we are doing when we refuse to admit the desires which take the shape of a poem, a play, a novel.

If, in fact, art is the human form of desire, then a world without art is one in which desire takes on inhuman, distorted forms. This is the argument we find in D. H. Lawrence's discussion of pornography and obscenity. For Lawrence, the really obscene attitude is the one which erects a standard of purity in sexual matters. It is obscene because it distorts, by denying, a fundamental human desire. It follows from his argument that those who would censor or inhibit art in the name of purity are the immoralists. The argument seems to me more valuable than the traditional ones urged against censorship, the argument concerned with the intent of the artist, for example. The traditional argument assumes and admits a morality which the work is in fact trying to subvert, that is, a morality which in the name of the good would deny the good, or rather what is beyond good or evil.

If we say that art is the human form of desire, we say that it is the vision of our complete humanity and an affirmation of love. Again, the argument depends on seeing the distorted and inhuman forms of a world without imagination. I am tempted to call the distrust of the imagination the Gulliver syndrome because Swift's Gulliver is the epitome of the unimaginative man and because nowhere else in literature do we see with more terrible clarity the consequences of the unimaginative life. Moving always amid abstractions, Gulliver concerns himself with system and structure rather than with being, and his desperate journey toward the good life is a journey deeper into the heart of darkness because of his refusal to accommodate himself to the burden he carries always with him, his own body. It is because Gulliver is unable to come to terms with himself that he can offer to the King of Brobdingnag the gift of European wisdom, gunpowder, and can describe its powers and effects, the devastating destruction of human beings, without so much as realizing for a moment what it is that he is describing. This, as more than one critic has noticed, is precisely the position of an Eichmann who, living amid the abstractions of clerical and administrative arrangements, effectively blinds himself to the horrors for which these arrangements are designed. It is because Gulliver cannot reconcile the abstractions he believes to be the means to utopia with the insistent presence of the human body which will not yield to abstraction that he finally can see the human being only as a filthy, degraded and horrifying being, the Yahoo. And it is from his position in a stable, among horses, that Gulliver pronounces his judgment on his fellow human beings, cursing them for the very blindness which afflicts him. In Gulliver's diatribe we hear the voice of the censor, the authentic accents of the moralist, the man who despises and hates mankind and who will have nothing to do with the vision of completed desire which might make him into a human being. From his stable, in the neighing accents of a horse, he calls down his contempt on the being who will not abide by the impossible denial of life that is in his words. He is a partial being, a man who walks like a horse, who tries to talk like a horse, who faints at the smell of human beings, who offers us a partial view of human life. And he has arrived here simply because he is partial, confusing the world of the intellect with the good life.

But insofar as art is wish or desire it is a good deal more than the patterns that the intellect can construct for us. Between the abstractions of mind and the perceptions of imagination there is and always will be an unholy gap. Criticism itself, confronted by the work of literature, confronted by the immediate perceptions which are the forms of desire, more often than not finds itself without a voice. The direct perception of a work of literature is, after all, something quite different from the intellectual system which the critic tries to construct to explain what it is that he has confronted. And it might be that more than a little of the confusion about the nature of the work of art, its meaning for us as human beings and as members of society, is the result of the ineptness of criticism in the face of the art it tries to defend and explain. Just as the unimaginative man takes on the form that his partial vision is creating, so an unimaginative criticism becomes partial and distorted as well. And not the least of its distortions is a shrinking back from the full implications of the work with which it is engaged. It might, for example, insist that the dream of art is, if not anarchic, simply the heaven beloved of theologians, or the contents of the unconscious postulated by depth-psychologists, anything but a marvellously direct perception of things as they are. Yet it is only when art moves among things as they are, which is of course, the mystery of things, that it speaks to us at all. This is the means by which it judges us, by recalling us again and again to the particular world in which we move and have our being, and by showing us the utter and terrible inhumanity and therefore immorality of the ghostly worlds we build when we separate ourselves from desire, from our imaginative perception of reality.

VII

CRITICISM AND SOCIETY

God's Spy

In one of his many guises the literary critic presents himself to us as custodian of social values. Since this is a weighty and responsible task, it calls for a substantial citizen, a portly fellow given to ponderous and magisterial pronouncements. After all, he carries a double load, both an unwieldy social structure and a rag-bag of literary tradition, and we cannot expect him to be nimble or graceful under that burden. Small wonder then that the least satisfying criticism is the very kind which we would hope might be most valuable, the kind we can call sociological criticism.

On the face of it, there seems no insurmountable problem facing the sociological critic. In the broadest sense, literature must in some way either affirm, express, reflect, or criticize social values, and presumably any analytic scheme that covered these terms would be an exhaustive one. Even the barbarians who reject society, we might say, serve a social purpose. I have heard it claimed that so-called subversive works in fact are a kind of Saturnalia in which socially unacceptable emotions and desires are expressed and in this way purged. Sometimes it seems as if the classrooms have become just this sort of carnival where, with a grand sneer at the social world in general, one can indulge in an orgy of subversive reading: *Catcher in the Rye, Coney Island of the Mind, The Opening of the Field,* all the contemporary works of anarchist and Zen Buddhist persuasion can be used as texts for sermons on the evils of society and therefore as safety valves for the pressures of anti-social attitudes.

I think that so long as one works within the context of social values, criticism will be confined to precisely such conclusions, and they are clearly trivial. In its least subtle form sociological criticism consists, whether it is concerned with affirmation or social nihilism, of a series of abstract and general notions applied in a haphazard manner to works taken as texts for sermons. On the one side, society itself can be understood only as an abstraction, however powerfully we may be aware of its presence in the form of sanction and law. On the other side, literature understood in social terms can only offer us either the flavour of social reality or its own embodiment of society, which we ought never to mistake for the real thing. To see what is meant here, one need only canvass those critical studies in which literature is interpreted sociologically, either as something caused by society or expressing it.

We are told, for example, by one of our best critics, that Canadian writers have a different sense of space and time from those writers in smaller, older countries, and that this tends to show itself in the way in which objects get jammed into the foreground of huge perspectives and in the ease with which we move through time so that all traditions of writing are available to us at once. We are told that fear of empty spaces dominates our writing, and that therefore terror is a key theme. We are told that colonialism, materialism, puritanism, the frontier mentality, all combine to produce in our writers a characteristic timidity and parochialism. We are told that the huge nation to our south draws out the life blood of our economy, leaving us with such pale and tired blood that we can only write pallid novels and anaemic verse. We are told that there are too many Anglo-Saxons, or too many French, or too many second-generation eastern European children here, and that we therefore lack a sense of identity. The list is one I could develop at length to show how easily explanations in general terms about a general subject offer themselves to the critic and how such explanations serve cheap purposes. In the end, after all, there is little sense or meaning in the statement that certain social conditions produced a given work. Nor is there much more sense in the opposite version: that a given work illuminates or comments on certain social conditions.

I am reminded that one Canadian critic assures us that if we listen closely to the poets in his anthology, we will catch the sound of the great Niagara falling, and hearing this, I am not surprised to find later in his discussion the argument that most of our verse is manly because Canadians are for the most part descendants of army officers.

A more subtle form of sociological criticism, of course, would insist on a more accurate, that is, intensive and thorough, account of social conditions, social structure, and social values as the standard for its work. But in this event the conclusion is inevitable, that literature itself either avoids the very problems with which this criticism is concerned or that it fails miserably in its attempt to express these problems. This is the exact conclusion, and the only possible conclusion one suspects, reached in John Porter's brilliant study of Canadian society. "The idea of class differences", writes Porter, "has scarcely entered into the stream of Canadian academic writing despite the fact that class differences stand in the way of implementing one of the most important values of western society, that is equality". And then buried decently in a footnote we find this: "Nor does class appear as a theme in Canadian literature." (*The Vertical Mosaic*, 1966, p. 6.) I would have been surprised at any other conclusion.

The point is that when we describe literature in social terms we tend at once to turn it into an imitative rather than a formative art, and we throw over it the shadow of illusion. By its very nature as a social imitation, literature becomes a secondary, caused phenomenon, and invariably it can be criticized as incomplete or partial because it can never hope to contain within it the social order which it imitates. From this point of view, literary works begin to look like pale, shrunken versions of society itself, and the writer becomes a timid provincial who reflects in the shadows of his writing the greater reality about him. A favourite sport of some critics illustrates the same point. Viewed historically, as an account of history and the development of a society, the Bible is a chaotic mess. It takes little acumen to show that it is filled with contradictions, that its social terminology is inaccurate and inadequate, that it obviously has been falsified to serve the purposes of kings and priests, and so on. And surely, to take another example, there are less clumsy ways of telling us about the Puritan revolution than the one Milton chose in writing *Paradise Lost*.

But, we may argue, if it is gross to seek for meaningful social comment in the content of literature, it still remains that the forms of literature are socially conditioned, if not socially determined. Ian Watt's account of the novel, for example, shows how the concept of character is determined by both philosophic empiricism and economic individualism, and there is no doubt that the highly individualized characters of a novel do differ from the diagrams of a morality play. And surely it might be said that the anti-utopia, say *Brave New World*, or *1984*, is a form appropriate to the development of scientific technology and totalitarianism in the twentieth century, and we can understand these fully only in the context of the society in which they took their shape. Aside from the fact that the argument does little to explain the occurrence of earlier, highly individualized characters in literature, or the anti-utopian form of say Swift's *Gulliver's Travels*, from which in fact Orwell derived some of his major patterns, it does not solve the problem that literary forms occur only in literature and are not found outside of it. In *1984*, for example, the major structural feature, whatever its content, is the ironic play of illusion and reality. Here in a stunning display of bitter reversals, Orwell presents us with a social structure that bases itself entirely on illusion, on the principles that lies are truth, that war is peace, that freedom is slavery, and against that massive illusion he places the baffled and thwarted human personality in the form of a shadowy creature trying desperately to find the means by which he might realize himself. Tested against the illusions of a mighty state, the values of the individual which we would want to affirm seem no more than shadows, the blind groping of the human being amid fragments of memory and desire. The ultimate nightmare of Orwell's story is that the illusion has become the reality, the state or society has finally swallowed the human personality, and the two distinguishing marks of humanity, language and love, have been perverted, one into the non-sense language of the state, the other into a sick desire to worship hatred and power. Far from being a socially determined form, Orwell's *1984* ironically detaches itself from society by insisting with terrible vehemence on the utter inhumanity of the illusion that presents itself as a form of humanity. We do not even know that Big Brother exists. We only see Winston Smith, a broken rag of a man, slobbering sentimentally over his love for the master.

We may say, then, that *1984* tells us it is possible to distinguish between humanity and society, that the social order is always less than human, always a diminishing of potentiality rather than a realization of potentiality. Irving Howe extends the distinction – or one like it – to all political novels. He tells us that the political novel exhibits a characteristic tension between the public element and what he calls the pastoral element, between "a sense of the rigors, necessities, and attractions of political life" and a characteristically apolitical temptation, usually something implied by the richness of human experience which will not yield to the abstractions of ideology. (*Politics and the Novel*, 1957, p. 23.)

Society, like politics, becomes a formal element of literature, not a cause of it. If we think of the tension between public and private elements in literature, it is easy to see the political or social version as only one version, and a disguised version at that, of the tension we find in all literature. We can say the social form is a disguised version of the more fundamental one, that is, the tension between literature and everything else we try to turn it into. The tension is simply the means by which the work insists on its autonomy, or if we prefer, its imaginative reality. Society may very well be an imperious necessity (to use Irving Howe's fine term here), but then necessity takes various forms: it may be the law of the gods, it may be the inscrutable working of a mechanical universe, it may be theory of evolution, it may be a tribal code of revenge, it may be dialectical materialism, or it may be the curse uttered by a wicked witch. Whether we give it social status, say the conventions of a puritanical society, or metaphysical status, say the will of God, or mythical status, the prophecy of an oracle, it is that against which the imagination forms itself and by means of which it attempts to release a vision of itself. Images of prison, of demonic cities, of narrow and confined communities, of parental figures, of tyrants, and of inscrutable and mysterious utterances from above are all appropriate to society as it is imagined in literature precisely because it is a version of law and necessity, as opposed to imaginative freedom which will take its shape in something quite different: more often than not a human community beyond law, or a divine city, or even a marriage which mocks the aged man who attempted to oppose it.

Characteristically, writers will carry over from literature to social comment their sense that the imagination opposes all forms of abstract rule and order, and they may then sound like social critics, either committing themselves to a particular program of social action which opposes the present structure, or even to a revolutionary program. But as Malraux saw so acutely in *Man's Fate*, even the commitment to the imperatives of history or to revolutionary action cannot reconcile the unholy gap between action and being. It is this gap which torments his hero Kyo, who learns finally that to love is more beautiful than to judge, and it is this gap which drives the assassin Ch'en to his demonic attempt to find a bridge. The only way in which Ch'en can fuse his divided being is to become the murder weapon himself, dying with his victim. The image is one which Browning used again and again: the demonic parody of the imaginative grasp of reality is murder, the exact antithesis of love. But if revolution is ultimately murderous and therefore the opposite of imagination, the writer cannot be a revolutionary, nor can he be committed to programs of social reform. He is rather the rebel, one who disengages himself from law and necessity in order to achieve imaginative freedom. The appropriate image here is not the image of the social critic but the image of the tramp, the irresponsible one, the one to whom all things are possible because nothing is forbidden. In a marvellous flash of insight, James Agee saw at once the gaiety and infantilism of the tramp figure, and understood that his ultimate subversiveness consisted not in a revolutionary threat to social order but in a disregard of order as complete as a child's.

At the beginning of a *Death in the Family*, the young Rufus watches the Chaplin figure on a flickering movie screen, watches as the graceful, finicky little man plays out forbidden sexual fantasies, dirties himself on eggs he has hidden in his trousers, and to the dismay of the boy and the delight of the adults, marches off on his dusty road, delicately and gingerly plucking at his trousers' seat.

Delight itself, we might be tempted to say, is subversive. But this is to stop too soon. What the imagination tries to release in its conflict with law is something more than an anti-social vision and something more than a moral vision. At the same time, it is something more than the merely personal, that is, feelings or emotions and their expressions. Martin Buber remarks that if institutions are "an animated clod without a soul", feelings are no more than "an uneasily fluttering soul bird", and he goes on to say that while many realize that "institutions yield no public life", only a few understand that "feelings yield no personal life". A true community would not arise from the loosening of the bonds of the mechanical state, nor out of the wish of people to live together through feelings of love for one another, but, in Buber's terms, only through "their taking their stand in living mutual relation with a living Centre". (*I and Thou*, 1958, pp. 44-45.) Buber's terms are essentially theological, but I take it they could be applied to theories of imaginative perception of reality.

There are other ways in which this could be put. Everything speaks to the writer in the language of his own being, essentially, I think, in the language of his body. The world as he views it, is neither law nor order nor abstract rule, but the world's body which is also his own, and it tells him, when he pays it the attention it demands and deserves, who and what he is. There is a poem by the Greek poet Odysseus Elytis which tells us of this union between the poet and the world and something of its consequences too; it is called "The Autopsy":*

And so, they found that the gold of the olive-root had dripped
into the recesses of his heart

And from many times he had lain awake by candle light waiting for
the dawn, a strange heat had seized his entrails

A little below the skin, the blue line of the horizon sharply painted
And ample traces of blue throughout his blood

---

* From *Six Poets of Modern Greece*, chosen, translated, and introduced by Edmund Keeley and Philip Shearrard, published by Thames and Hudson and copyright in 1960 by Authors (Camelot Press Ltd., London).

The cries of the birds which he had come to memorize in hours of
great loneliness apparently spilled out all at once, so that it
was impossible for the knife to enter deeply

Probably the intention sufficed for the evil

Which he met — it is obvious — in the terrifying posture of the innocent,
his eyes open, proud, the whole forest moving still on the unblemished
retina.

Nothing in the brain but the dead echo of the sky

Only in the hollow of the left ear some fine light sand, as though
in a shell. Which means that he often walked by the sea alone with
the pain of love and the roar of the wind.

As for those particles of fire on his thighs, they show that he
moved time hours ahead whenever he embraced a woman

We shall have early fruit this year.

When we dissect the poet's body, Elytis tells us, we find it is
the world's body, or rather that he was made of his perceptions
of the world, and of something else as well: some kind of passion,
love, innocence, that has done peculiar things to time itself and
that bears in it the seeds of growth and fruition.

The terrifying posture of the innocent: I think the phrase
does justice to the challenging naïveté of the writer, a naïveté
which expresses itself in his refusal to do anything but obey the
demands of his perceptions. And this seems to me the crux. To
obey in the most literal-minded fashion one's perceptions and to
accept only one's perceptions is, in social terms certainly, naïve.
Nine-tenths of our social energies are expended in a massive
effort to convince ourselves that what is totally apparent is not
at all true. I think this is what Orwell means, for example, when
he tells us that political language is bad language because it
must tell lies, and it is certainly what his paradigm of power
shows us: sanity is statistical, not perceptual. One thinks again
of Huck Finn who is driven to precisely the inversions which
Orwell explores: if his society is telling the truth, then he will
be a liar; if it has the keys to the kingdom of heaven, then he will
go to hell; if it is good, then his only course is to be wicked; and
what drives him to these apparently demonic conclusions is that
the witness of his seeing eyes, his love, and his sympathy con-

tradict everything which has been told to him and told to him and told to him. And he is, after all, only a boy.

Perhaps the writer's perception comes down simply to his refusal to be taken in. Perhaps only to his stubborn adherence to the simplest of maxims: Change yourself, or, Nothing matters but life itself. Truisms, no doubt. But they are denied, perverted, twisted with savage and terrible intent and effect whenever we substitute for them any one of those thousand abstractions which come so easily and glibly to our lips; when, for example, we substitute for perception, the spectres of time or space or consequences or state or society.

The critic who presents himself to us as a custodian of social values turns out to be on the side of law as opposed to imagination. He may be able to tell us much about law, though on the whole I would rather listen to an expert in law than a critic on this subject. He may be able to tell us much about social custom and the habits of the tribe, though one suspects a sociologist will have more to say than he can. He may be able to assure us of the ways in which literature improves the quality of our lives or enriches our moments of leisure or even loosens the bonds of the mechanical state, but more often than not he will warn us away from frivolous and irresponsible work. In any event, so long as he is concerned with the social values of literature, it is certain he will not be able to tell us anything at all about the imagination, or the ways in which it works, or the reasons why we might without fear give ourselves to that world which is, without question, not the one we find in our society.

THE FUNCTION OF CRITICISM
AT THE PRESENT TIME

The Silent Speaking Words

"Poets are always celebrating the burning of libraries", remarks Karl Shapiro in an introduction to Henry Miller's *Tropic of Cancer* (1961, p. xii). Critics, we might be tempted to say, are always trying to build libraries. If there is anything at all to this distinction, it is that it reminds us of one made by John Stuart Mill in his essay on Bentham and Coleridge, a distinction between, as he put it, "the worshippers of Civilization and of Independence, of the present and of the remote past". On the question of "how far mankind have gained by civilization", Mill observes we can suppose two thinkers entirely at variance with one another:

"One observer is forcibly struck by the multiplication of physical comforts; the advancement and diffusion of knowledge; the decay of superstition; the facilities of mutual intercourse; the softening of manners . . . the progressive limitation of the tyranny of the strong over the weak"; another is struck by "the relaxation of individual energy and courage; the loss of proud and self-relying independence; the slavery of so large a portion of mankind to artificial wants . . . the sufferings of the great mass of the people of civilized countries, whose wants are scarcely better provided for than those of the savage, while they are bound by a thousand fetters", and this one, far from "worshipping our enlightened age", may "be apt to infer that savage life is preferable to civilized; that the work of civilization should as far as possible be undone." (*Mill on Bentham and Coleridge*, 1950, pp. 105-106.)

But it is equally possible to turn this around and to make the critic of present civilization not a worshipper of savagery but of a literate past which must be revived or somehow once more brought effectively into our lives. There may be something to be said, after all, for building libraries rather than burning them. Many of us, surely, would feel that the burning of books is barbaric. We might associate it with lurid scenes from the not so distant past: storm troopers on a night of the long knives dancing around the flames of burning books in Berlin, a fire soon to be succeeded by other, more sinister flames. Remembering that, we might turn to the critic with new respect. Here is the one who preserves the heritage of the past, who hands on to us the best that has been known and thought, who refuses to be blinded by the present, but who rather ranges across the centuries to seek out what is worth our care. Having removed himself from the clamorous traffic of the present and the insistent demands of an energetic society to destroy whatever stands in its way, he alone, free of the vertigo induced by the whirl of action in which we find ourselves, tells us to cherish rather than obliterate our own memories.

We have two possibilities, then: the critic as savage or the critic as conservative. Most modern criticism takes its form from two brilliant conservatives, Arnold and Coleridge. It was Arnold who formulated against a background of growing barbarism a major statement of what F. R. Leavis calls "the general function of critical intelligence in a civilized community" ("Introduction" to *Mill on Bentham and Coleridge*, p. 38), and it was Coleridge who introduced to criticism in its modern form a theory of symbolism and therefore a critical concern with meaning. From Arnold, modern criticism gets its sense of detachment and disinterestedness, its feeling for lucidity and flexibility, its concern for a structure of values, and especially for the value of criticism as the free play of intelligence over its materials. From Coleridge, it gets its sense of the organic nature of art, its opposition to mechanism of any sort, its psychological keenness. And from both, its desire to become knowledge and system.

Arnold, no doubt, was unduly fastidious. Poetry being what it is, there are times when criticism must get its hands dirty. And Coleridge, as everyone knows, loved cloudy metaphysical distinctions of the Germanic sort. But still, between them, Arnold and Coleridge charted out the possibilities of criticism for a hundred years to follow. They broke out of the limitations of neo-classic imitative theory and enabled criticism to engage for the first time fully and completely with the complexities of the creative personality. They distinguished in detail between limited social ends and the ideals of culture. They offered the means for a new structuralism and thus a general theory. Above all, they set the tone for criticism as we now know it: intelligent, perceptive, humanistic, inclusive, and conservative. Neither would ally himself with the modern temper of liberalism nor with its radical individualism.

Whatever its philosophic basis, conservative criticism must ultimately seek to explain, interpret, evaluate, and formalize literature. Its urge is systematic, though that might seem a curious adjective to apply to a temper like Coleridge's, and though it might seem to be at odds with the conservative resistance to explicit rational formulations. The apparent paradox here is resolved easily enough, for the reason that conservative criticism must postulate a tradition and a body of literature which in its own way is formative. Perhaps the clearest version of it is Arnold's own when he tells us that criticism is finally concerned with an intellectual order, an order of ideas of which the creative power might profitably avail itself. And it is particularly this rational urge, this intellectualism, to which I want to draw attention here. Whatever we make of Arnold's flexibility and taste or of his sense of the powers of a free criticism, it is an intellectual freedom, an intellectual flexibility, and even an intellectual taste of which he is speaking. This is what accounts for the awesome apparatus of learning which has accumulated about modern criticism. This too accounts for the peculiar jargon in which it tends to express itself: a jargon which suggests criticism is constantly striving toward the condition of science and more than likely social science. It also tells us why poems tend to sound, in the accounts which we get of them from modern critics, either like complicated philosophic and semantic arguments or disguised versions, and learned ones at that, of anthropological studies or comparative mythology.

There is no doubt that as intellectual criticism, as a theory of literature, society, morality, or what have you, modern criticism represents an impressive achievement. It is as close to a satisfactory systematic criticism as has ever been reached, and its links with other disciplines of thought are well-founded and soundly worked out. But its effects, if we are to judge it by these alone, are disturbing. One has only to read the scholarly journals to understand this. Once the stronghold of literary scholarship, these have now become the territory of the young critics who exercise there the techniques of the new intellectualism, and it is difficult to imagine a drearier wasteland than the one they have created. With a persistence frightening to watch, they pursue work after work until it has been corralled, roped, castrated, branded, and shoved out with the rest of the herd: this one relegated to the field of archetypes, that one to ambiguity, the other to paradox, and the prize specimens to the centre ring to be displayed as the folklore of the industrial age. What we are watching, it seems to me, is the ferociousness of the intellect turned loose on the beasts of the field, and it seems to me a ferociousness peculiar to our age. It is a ferociousness, for example, which we can see elsewhere: in the terrifying energy with which we devote ourselves to the race to the moon, or in the energy with which we construct new universities or rip apart the centres of cities to thrust up there higher and higher buildings. One can imagine how appalled Arnold would have been to see this intellectual ferocity applied to social ends. There is a sense in which he foresaw what would happen. He records it in one exceptional poem, the *Stanzas from the Grande Chartreuse*, though he believed it was the practical intelligence and not the critical which would effect the changes we are now seeing. It may be that his analysis is correct, but the point surely is that the separation of intellect from immediate human activity frees it in a peculiar way and leads to peculiar and frightening ends. In any event, confident as he was in his critical essays that the disinterested intellect was necessary to criticism, in his own poetry Arnold spoke with another voice. There, knowing that man in his practical activities is a slave, Arnold sought for lucidity, plainness, and freedom, for a detachment which would let him be *in* but not *of* the world. Yet, and this I think was the

68

source of his profound melancholy, he knew that such detachment was purchased at a price, the price of lassitude, of a kind of despair which comes from the awful paradox that in action we are sometimes less than human but unless we are involved in life we are remote and icy beings. It was the buried life for which he sought in his poetry though he feared it might be madness.

And this, I believe, is the question facing the critic today when he asks himself, as he must, what he ought to do; when, as Arnold himself puts it, he seizes "an occasion for trying his own conscience", and when he attempts to discover "of what real service . . . the practice of criticism either is or may be made to his own mind and spirit and to the mind and spirit of others". If the conservative function of criticism has unleashed a destructive intellectualism, is the alternative simply savagery? If the poet celebrates the burning of libraries, does this mean that today the critic can and must become a book-burner as well? And in what way could an orgy of book-burning be better than a destructive intellectualism?

One answer, of course, is to point out that the book-burning poet is not really an enemy of poetry but of the enshrined books of the tradition which we so easily decide to call literature. If he puts himself against society, he also puts himself against literature, that is, an establishment, an orthodoxy, a limitation. As often as not, in fact, he will build another library to put in place of the one he has just burned down. Ezra Pound was just such a book-burner and so is Karl Shapiro. In fact, it is the canonized tradition to which he is taking such violent exception, and he promptly replaces it with another, a list which I personally find both remarkable and attractive. Not, he says, "Milton, Marlowe, Pope, Donne", but "Dostoevsky, Kurt Hamsun, Strindberg, Nietzsche . . . Fauré, Spengler . . . Rimbaud, Ramakrishna, Blavatsky, Huysmans, Count Keyserling, Prince Kropotkin, Lao-Tse, Nostradamus, Petronius, Rabelais". And still others: Carroll, Chesterton, Conrad, Cooper, Emerson, Rider Haggard, Henty,—Joyce, Machen, Mencken, Cowper Powys, Spencer, Thoreau, Whitman, Goldman, and Twain. (*Tropic of Cancer*, pp. xi-xii.) But this is merely a game. Anyone can construct lists of anti-traditions, especially esoteric and pop-art ones. The critic as book-burner and savage is something more than a new traditionalist, though his frivolity and irresponsibility are essential to his character.

Unlike the civilized man who moves amid ideas and abstractions, the savage moves only amid perceptions; and presumably where the civilized man has learned that maturity involves the ability to postpone and substitute for immediate satisfaction, the savage, knowing nothing of future or past, seeks only for gratification of desire. These are not historical or psychological observations, but literary ones. They refer to modes of thinking and feeling about poetry rather than to actual states of being, and are no more real than Mill's two thinkers with whom we began. Presumably the literal and historical savage is a degraded being, and certainly so far as contemporary anthropology has been able to tell us, he is anything but the representative of Independence as opposed to Civilization. Like the child in literature, the savage or the clown or the fool is a symbol. He is, at least in some of his manifestations, what Leslie Fiedler would call an Id figure. He appears as the image of all that is irrational in the human being: revelry and misrule, gluttony and mischief, folly and trickery, cunning and simple-mindedness. And it is precisely this which the civilized and cultivated man is not prepared to admit into his life, unless only in the few holidays he will allow himself, and then only in the most cautious and disguised way. But if there is any sense at all in which art is an expression of irrational urges, the desire of man, it follows that the civilized or cultivated approach to art will invariably either turn it into an illusion or into an intellectual structure. As the language of the body, anarchic, grotesque, ludicrous, art remains an illusion to the intellect and a threat to the intellect and to the ordering powers of man. To what then is it accessible?

The question here really is whether it is possible to have a criticism which is irrational, which moves amid perceptions, which does not attempt to impose on individual works or on art itself a structure of reason or indeed a pattern of any kind except that of perception. One difficulty is that perceptions do appear as anarchic. To that gentle and wonderful humanist Santayana, Robert Browning seemed to be a barbarian because

Browning could never forget that he had an appetite, because it was experience alone which he seemed to value. And Browning, master of the grotesque, is also master of a world in which the general and abstract has no meaning. Perhaps as clearly as any writer Browning saw that the wisdom of the body, if it could be said to have any wisdom at all, extended to so limited an area of experience that it could hardly have anything to say to a society, or to a culture, or to anything so august as a civilization. He saw that in its limitations the human body is ludicrous and grotesque. But he saw as well that it was only in terms of these limitations (he called it the imperfect) that man could be understood, and that in art, as in religion, and as in personal life, the only meaning of which we can speak is the meaning of the perceived moment. In that, there is a theory of creativity, a theory which unites or fuses the critic with the work of art, just as the artist must fuse himself with his material before it becomes meaningful. Like Henry James, Browning would say there are no facts, there are only interpretations, or even better, there are only perceptions.

The Ring and the Book, like James's masterpiece of ambiguity, *The Turn of the Screw*, and like a contemporary version of the same theme, Truman Capote's *In Cold Blood*, explores a murderous world of abstractions in which evil takes on shapes that leave one appalled, and at the same time suggests that as opposed to abstractions, perceptions open out not on murder but love. When this happens, when the world is seen in its fully realized human terms, then we discover the choice we are being given is between judgment and mercy, between justice and love, and that the two are not complementary, but opposed.

The critic as savage, then, is not merely the irrationalist, though, of course, he puts himself against rationalism and its methods in criticism. He is not concerned with interpretation, or with explanation, or with evaluation. He does not want to judge but to participate in, to become one with the work of literature. The establishment, the vested interests of criticism, of course, will raise a howl at this suggestion. It smacks, we will be told, of impressionism, of the decadence of Walter Pater and his re-creation of artistic experience. It is, we will be told, mere subjectivity and therefore anarchic. It takes away the one possibility of agreed-on critical procedures and so makes the Ph.D. examinations almost impossible to set and certainly impossible to grade. I am not sure that the charges are altogether unjust. An irrational criticism concerned with sympathetic participation in literature rather than with detached examination and evaluation is undoubtedly subjective and unsystematic; by the canons of the hard-headed amongst our conservatives it is probably sentimental as well. One can hear the ghost of Wyndham Lewis raising again the most inhuman cry ever raised in literary criticism, that concern with perceptions is the concern of the dumb ox. But, it seems to me, at the present time—and it is the function of criticism at the present time of which we are speaking—criticism must risk the excesses of subjectivity and sentimentality if it is going to become human once more and if it is going to bring us closer to the unsolved mystery at the heart of all our best perceptions. It is no longer Arnold and Coleridge and Eliot who have anything important to say to us but rather Browning and Pound, Lawrence, Orwell, Agee, and Miller: anti-intellectuals, irrationalists, angry men, and writers who knew how much of themselves they had to give in order that they might be able to say anything at all as critics. The rationale of such criticism, I would suggest, might be found in the first book of Browning's *Ring and the Book*, in James's critical prefaces, and in the astonishing meditations on art in Agee's *Let Us Now Praise Famous Men*. The choice would seem to be between a universe of death opened out to us by the mind and intellect of man, and a living world into which, through our perceptions, we might finally enter.

At the centre of Tennyson's *In Memoriam*, in the 95th lyric of that long threnody for Arthur Hallam, the poet experiences a vision. He has for some time attempted to understand the meaning of death both in personal terms and in terms of the precise knowledge of his time, and he has discovered only that as an individual in an empirically conceived world, he must view the world as a wasteland, God as a snake, and himself as a walking corpse. Now through the exercises of his grief and through his absorption in a poetic meditation on his friend's being, he comes to the lawn of the rectory where he lives. There, alone, in the night, he reads the letters of his friend:

A hunger seized my heart; I read
Of that glad year which once had been
In those fallen leaves which kept their green,
The noble letters of the dead.

And strangely on the silence broke
The silent-speaking words, and strange
Was love's dumb cry defying change
To test his worth; and strangely spoke

The faith, the vigour, bold to dwell
On doubts that drive the coward back,
And keen thro' wordy snares to track
Suggestion to her inmost cell.

So word by word, and line by line,
The dead man touch'd me from the past
And all at once it seem'd at last
The living soul was flash'd on mine. . . .

This is one of the most penetrating passages in all literature: there is not a lie in it, yet it tells us what we can scarcely bring ourselves to believe, that words which are silent can speak, that love defies change, and that through words and lines the poet was touched by the dead man. Whatever we make of it, we do know that for Tennyson the world had changed: the wasteland had become a garden; the snake-God a father; and the walking corpse a living soul; but not through reason or system or intellect. The miracle, if it was such, happened word by word and line by line, through the language and vision of poetry whose words, Tennyson tells us, are silent-speaking words. Beyond system, this is where criticism finally must go: to the paradoxical speech of poetry that tells us all when it speaks to us, as the critic must learn to do, in silence.